THE MATURE
ENTREPRENEUR

THE MATURE ENTREPRENEUR

Prosper after Retirement

Copyright © 2021 by Eitan Litvin

All rights reserved. This book or any part of it thereof shall not be reproduced or used in any manner whatsoever without the express written permission of the publisher except for the use of brief quotations in a book review or scholarly article.

Printed in the United States of America

THE MATURE ENTREPRENEUR

PROSPER AFTER **RETIREMENT**

EITAN LITVIN

CONTENTS

INTRODUCTION 1

CHAPTER ONE | *The Message* 3

CHAPTER TWO | *Gabby's Fashion Story* 8

CHAPTER THREE | *Natalie: The Book Company Owner For Kids* 13

CHAPTER FOUR | *David's Family Services Story* 18

CHAPTER FIVE | *About Ellen Langer's Youth Primes* 22

CHAPTER SIX | *Marco's Photography Story* 25

CHAPTER SEVEN | *Karen's Friendly Face Story* 29

CHAPTER EIGHT | *Eva's Bags And Belts Design Story* 37

CHAPTER NINE | *Jacob's Web Content Writing Tale* 43

CHAPTER TEN | *Betty's Special Coffee Story* 49

CHAPTER ELEVEN | *Rachel's Outsourcing Office Services Story* 56

CHAPTER TWELVE | *Lisa's Personal Chef Story* 63

CHAPTER THIRTEEN | *Elsa Ebay Sales Story* 69

CHAPTER FOURTEEN | *Judith's Jewelery Story* 76

CHAPTER FIFTEEN | *Nadine Bookkeeping Services Story* 83

CHAPTER SIXTEEN | *Alex's 'S Private Teaching Story* 86

CHAPTER SEVENTEEN | *Flora Soap Making Story* 90

CHAPTER EIGHTEEN | *Bert's Story As A Family Historian* 93

CHAPTER NINETEEN | *Nancy's Consulting Story* 97

CHAPTER TWENTY | *Donna's Story Of Patchwork Quilts Couture* 100

CHAPTER TWENTY-ONE | *Alfred's Story: A Research Using The Internet* 104

CHAPTER TWENTY-TWO | *The Story Of Cyril's Youth Care* 113

CHAPTER TWENTY-THREE | *Wrap Up* 116

INTRODUCTION

Welcome, you have just made an amazing first step, into entrepreneurship and how to make the most success of it.

Dear reader, we may never have met, but because you picked this book, there is something about you that you may not have shared with anyone in the past. I guess there is something burning in your bones with a latent or overt desire for you to do what you longed for.

Today you will have the opportunity to realize a dream that has been alive within you for a long time. A dream that matters to you that will be realized.

This book will take you step by step through how to become an entrepreneur and start your own small business that offers services or goods, any type of business, manufacturing or trade.

The book will also feature a variety of ideas and true stories, from retirees who have started small businesses in manufacturing, sales, publishing, services and charities in various entrepreneurial fields.

This book is designed to be an inspiration to emulate their success.

Get out of your chair and do something you enjoy.

The first part of this book is an ongoing pep talk to greying readers to get out of their chairs, rethink their lives and do something they really enjoy that supplements their income, which is likely to be in short supply after leaving their regular work.

The book is written in such a way to help you start your own business, and can provide ideas not only to retirees but also to younger people who feel trapped in boring salaried jobs and want to start their own successful businesses.

You have the right to follow your dream and enjoy yourself.

Now is the time for a modern approach and a fresh way of thinking to accept and implement new ideas.

In this journey, you will enter a world characterized by action and an enlightened approach to a diverse and challenging life that is attainable, enjoyable, healthy and beneficial. This journey will fulfil your dreams.

You have the right to have fun.

CHAPTER ONE

THE MESSAGE

This is a clear call to all retirees to refuse to live in activities designed to spend time without challenges, or without ambitions and potential priorities for the rest of their lives.

We need goals that give us hope for a better future and the reason to continue living full, positive lives and doing something we enjoy day in and day out.

we must break from the routine and avoid living a monotonous life as society expects of us. We always have the ability and the strength to expand the boundaries that characterize our journey and to increase the number of opportunities we have.

We cannot ignore the fact that our physiological body is in decline and is less forgiving. But on the other hand, in our age, despite physical limitations, the mindset almost always beats reality.

What I mean is that almost anything can be determined by us. The ability to reformulate our universe gives us the ability to reject any collective consensus on what we should or should not be doing at such ages. We choose what we're going to do, and because we want to, we do it.

Entrepreneurship is a perfect way to spend your 50s, 60s, 70s and beyond.

I have spoken with many baby boomers' entrepreneurs; they all said they couldn't imagine retiring. Yes, they've slowed down, but owning a business gives them a sense of independence to be their own employer, to be the centre of their life and to realize that everything depends on them.

We cannot change the cards we have in this game of life, but we can certainly change the way we play those cards.

Today you don't have to compromise your situation; you can change your situation and conquer new heights.

> "The greatest danger for most of us is not that our goal is too high and we miss it, but that it is too low and we reach it."
> (Michelangelo)

In all respects, you deserve to change your condition.

To this day, considering your age, you must believe that you have not yet reached your full potential and pursue your aspirations that have not yet come true.

It is therefore with great enthusiasm that this book reaches you. The intention of this book is to uncover your experiences and open up possibilities you have never allowed yourself to dream of before.

PREVIEW

This section is an overview of the new post-retirement condition of baby boomers.

Population aging is the most critical demographic trend in Western countries, which means people are living longer and the number of people aged 65 and over in the general population is gradually increasing.

Today in the West, the population aged 65 and over constitutes about 12 percent of the total population. Experts expect this rate to reach a quarter (25%) of the total population within a decade.

Many of us, physically and emotionally, feel that it is too early to retire. Our minds are clear in the second half of our adult life and we are still active.

Life expectancy has been one of the most common topics in the medical literature over the past decades. The sociological aspects of this phenomenon are discussed at conferences; reports examine its effects.

This is one of the most challenging and important social phenomena of the twenty-first century. Never before have so many people had such a load of experience, knowledge, time and ability to contribute to the significant performance of the economy and to the society.

The problem is that the retiree is still viewed by individuals as an elderly man with no power. The origin of the image is that, regardless of his condition in the biological aging process or his subjective feeling, society defines the person as an old man at a certain chronological age. It is the product of a social consensus which is not anchored in medical science.

Creating new meaning and new content for our lives is the most significant challenge for us.

A life worth living and which, over time, guarantees good health and prosperity.

On the other hand, it is sad to see many people that retirement represents the beginning of their degeneration process.

The loss of shine in their eyes, the decline in vitality and the general degradation.

A life in which there is continued creativity, involvement in people's lives, renewed self-expression, a sense of accomplishment and appreciation is a life worth living and preventing burnout.

Along with our leisure and family, we need to develop space for new occupations and activities, based on a hobby, work or entrepreneurship platforms that provide an experience of creativity, involvement, self-expression, success, and appreciation.

You have retired and you are wondering,

What is happening now?

What is the Meaning of my Life?

These are not deep philosophical questions about practical things. In many situations, instead of responding to these issues, we sprinkle a_smokescreen as they bother us since retirement. The point is, each of us has the answers to those questions that are important to our happiness, there really is no need to wait for a moment of enlightenment to find the answers.

Continuing to live a good, meaningful and happy life is within our grasp.

To discover your meaning in your life, answer the following questions:

- What are the important things in my life?
- What legacy do I want to leave behind?
- What would I do if I had the power to change the world?

Reflection and Application: Find your purpose

Directly opposed to what some may believe, finding your purpose is achievable. Continuing to live a good, successful and happy life is within your reach.

Your answer to the questions below will help you live your daily life in accordance with your values. Before your own eyes, it will help you see your purpose unfold.

- What do you want to do in your life?
- Who are you?

- What are the important things in your life?
- What do you like to do more than anything else?
- What legacy would you like to leave behind?
- What would you do now if you knew you could not fail?
- If money and time were not a problem, what would you like to do more than anything else?
- What is your most enjoyable activity?
- What is the biggest challenge you have encountered in your life, are you willing to help other people overcome this challenge?
- Who are the people you respect and why are they respected by you?
- If you had the opportunity to go back in time, what career would you choose?
- What will your dream day be like?
- If you had the power to change the world, what would you do?
- What does your heart tell you to do?
- If you had three wishes for the same questions.

Take a notebook, scribble down your ideas and add your own useful questions

CHAPTER TWO

GABBY'S FASHION STORY

In different ways, business ideas will come to you; Mine started one day when my twelve-year-old granddaughter came to me with deeply moving tears and showed me her favourite jeans stained with ink. "Grandma, you have to save my jeans," my granddaughter pleaded. I knew from my past that there was no way to wipe off the ink stains, but before I could tell her the bitter truth, my granddaughter and her friends were gone, leaving me on a rescue mission.

I am a 70-year-old retiree; I have worked in our local town for over 35 years. I have dreamed of being a fashion designer all my life. Along with my designs of fashionable clothes and accessories, I have dozens of notebooks from another era in my life.

I told myself I couldn't disappoint my granddaughter, so I had the vision to draw flowers on the ink stains, incorporate studs, and transform traditional jeans into trendy pants. My granddaughter's confidence sparked my creative energy.

"Thank you, Grandma, you are the coolest", my granddaughter said that when I gave her the Revamped Jeans. She came to visit me the next day, flanked by two of her closest friends and their old jeans. They asked me to draw the same drawing and the same additions as my granddaughter. They told me that all the girls in their group wanted similar jeans to inspire me more.

My granddaughter then asked me, Grandma, why not start a business with your paintings and sell denim clothes? The more I think about it, the brighter the idea becomes. I have a lot of creative ideas for painting denim jeans, and I'm sure I'll take advantage of them.

The problem was, I didn't know how to start and maintain this kind of business. I turned to a consultant at the suggestion of a friend of mine who advised me and supported me during the first stages of setting up the business. I was able to foresee some of these problems and solve them with careful preparation.

Today I upgrade denim jeans in different stores across the country and also export painted denim to Europe. I hire two assistants; my livelihood thrives from the small business I started, and the work fills my life. My dreams come true, all because of my granddaughter's little inkblot in her denim.

GABBY'S TIP

- If the idea is right for you, if your gut feelings tell you, "Go ahead", this is the right step.
- Being an entrepreneur at our age allows us to keep our minds and bodies engaged.

Entrepreneurship Meaning After Retirement Age

In this chapter, we will discuss the importance of entrepreneurship after retirement age.

When you're your own boss, age discrimination doesn't really exist. The time of the "old entrepreneur" has already arrived with the large number of baby boomers already reaching retirement age. Age may have diminished our prospects for work, but we also have the economic capacity to start our own businesses with the possibility of pursuing a second career, doing everything we always wanted to do.

So, what do you do with all this time on your hands?

Watch TV? waste your time and money at the café shops or cinemas?

For individuals, institutions, and communities, the big problem is:

With these extra years, what are we going to do?

It's never too late to embark on an entrepreneurial journey.

Now is the time to start a new business. Age is an advantage that comes with experience, maturity and a solid circle of personal contacts, we bring skills with us. All of these are invaluable assets, and they are ours.

It's never too late to begin an entrepreneur's new journey unrelated to your chronological era.

> *Decisions Were Mainly the Product Of External Influences*

We're in a play that we haven't written or directed for much of our lives. In our youth, with no real-life experience, we made important decisions based on minimal knowledge. These decisions were mostly the product of external influences such as our parents, the society in which we lived, and the media. It takes a long time to grow up and achieve what we really want to do, and all of a sudden you find yourself in old age and behind us we see a career that we might not have had.

We are more confident, more experienced at our age, have more status and accomplishments, more connections, expertise and resources, and more likely to make the right choices.

Most of us have a better understanding of who we are at our age and what the world is like, and we can be credited with much more success than when we were younger.

The expertise we have gained includes possibilities that we did not have decades ago. Today, instead of blind optimism, abstract images and dreams, we can model our decisions on real data. Entrepreneurship is not just about making money; it is also a question of freedom and fulfilment. It's fantastic to fill the rest of our lives with a good entrepreneurial effort that will allow us to do that.

Think about your family, your children, your grandchildren, your friends, your surroundings, yourself, what really matters to you and how you want to be honoured.

Become an Entrepreneur

We have traditionally seen old age as the last stage in the life of those reaching their retirement years; this definition is obsolete - there is now a fourth age for the elderly. Senior citizens will live more than decades of fulfilling and productive lives because of technological advancement.

Active aging has now replaced the golden years, which means entrepreneurship is much more likely to be on the menu for people in their 50s, 60s and 70s.

Any new experience gives you a choice, and aging is no exception. If you choose to be inactive, old age will come to you and you will be easily drawn to gravity. But if you choose the way to create with happiness and fulfilment, you will delay aging and enjoy retirement.

The essence of senior entrepreneurship means different things to different individuals,

To be truly independent.

Pursuing their desires and passions. Start their own business because they always wanted to, but never had the chance.

Increase income.

Explore an idea for a new product or service that addresses a problem or responds to a consumer need.

Illustrate the entrepreneurial conduct that leads to gains for the community. Others volunteer to help community projects with their leadership and entrepreneurial skills.

Create their own business when they cannot find a daily job.

Invest, support and obtain great personal satisfaction from start-ups.

It is inevitable that more and more people will choose to become entrepreneurs later in life over the next decade. While achieving their goals, they will create jobs and stimulate growth. It will be extremely rewarding for them and good news for the economy.

For most economies, this increase in entrepreneurship in the third age is generally good news, as entrepreneurship leads to more innovation, increases in productivity, creates jobs and also contributes to growth and well-being in general.

Throughout this book, woven success stories tell the stories of customers, friends and acquaintances. The many entrepreneurial areas listed come from several selections of small businesses in manufacturing, sales, publishing, service and voluntary organizations.

A cluster that talks about the dilemmas, problems and questions that entrepreneurs faced when they started to set up their business, how they went about doing things, and in particular the courage to break down barriers on the way to realization are some of examples that are used here.

CHAPTER THREE

NATALIE: THE BOOK COMPANY OWNER FOR KIDS

"Hello! My name is Natalie, and this is my story of how I built a thriving business after I retired. When I was sixty-three, I retired from my long-term job and I felt upset and confused by my situation, I had already exhausted my retirement savings and in the meantime had no idea what was going on.

I consulted a professional consultant to help me discover myself. In a two-period investigation, he shot questions and answers at me like a tennis ball. The truth was, I didn't have the answers to the question posed to me during these sessions, but we could actually find out how experienced I was, how much I had never really been a professional. One thing that stood out of all the questioning was the way I love to raise and take care of my family.

At the end of my second session, my counsellor stood at the door, much like a scene from the TV series "Colombo" and asked me a key question: "What part of child care do you loved in particular?". With this question it became more and more evident that I have a passion for child care and storytelling. And at that time, my genuine source of happiness was taking care of my children and grandchildren. To tell them the stories I made up, the stories in which the protagonists of the tale were my children and grandchildren.

Then my consultant asked me what I thought about telling more children's stories and making money with them. I say it seems like the best idea in years. It was fantastic doing what I want to do naturally and making money from it. I continued my sessions for the next two months and finally decided on the opening of a children's bookstore.

I wrote about 25 stories to tell to children and grandchildren during the creation of the business. I hired the services of an illustrator to draw many figures in the stories. My husband, who was in charge of the book printing, was very supportive. My business eventually started selling children's books, and I changed the names of the heroes to the names of the children reading the novel. It's a whole new start that I never dreamed of or thought about in my life.

Now, five years after starting the business, I have already entrusted my daughter with the regular administration of the business, although I am the president of this business and mainly continues to nourish my story factory fuelled by heroes who read it. My story making facility is a late filming operation, a lifetime business with books translated into 20 languages and a global business model. It was a complete experience that I wish I had started earlier in my life. However, I appreciate that I took the step to make a difference in my life. "

NATALIE'S TIPS

- "You shouldn't have to know everything to start and run a small business, I recommend that you hire a professional, advisor or consultant.
- "Starting a business has helped me plan all aspects of my life while sharing my values and beliefs and creating a successful, fulfilling and successful culture,"

"Everything is in your Mind,"

This message demonstrates to skeptical individuals that, despite the dramatic increase in the life expectancy of our generation, many of us still struggle to understand and accept the fact that we still have enough time to make our dreams come true.

AGING IS EXPRESSED MAINLY IN THE WAY WE THINK, RATHER THAN THE WAY WE SEEM

Some time ago a young entrepreneur approached me to help him develop a sporting goods business. The 36-year-old business owner, a professional footballer, was forced to retire at the age of 36 and was already deemed too old for the game due to his age.

He told me there were players half his age on the team with him. Due to the player's experiences and advanced age, the young players on his team admired him. He told me that several of these young players had told him repeatedly that they couldn't imagine what it was like to be so old. Only in an 18-year-old will 36 appear "old".

I remember looking at 34–40-year-olds as an enormous achievement when I was 18 or 20, thinking that I would be so confident and educated then.

I didn't even dream of being 36 in the distant future either.

Including our age, everything is subjective. It is perhaps more important to focus on mindset rather than age.

IT'S MENTAL, "IT'S ALL IN YOUR MIND."

Without a doubt, at this point you are asking yourself, what should I do now?

I suggest you do the following;

- Show more curiosity and interest about what is going on around you
- Keep up to date with changes that are taking place at your own pace and implement them.
- Be inventive, cheerful, and use humor. Creativity, laughter and the love of life are proven tools for prolonging life; they often define the quality of your life.

- Accept that you are still relevant. Make a U-turn and follow the path parallel to that set for you in advance.

At the end of the alley, you may not find the Fountain of Youth, but you will find that you are still important and that it is your decision to take the right course.

> *"TO LIVE THE PAST IS A HOBBY THAT BECOMES AN OCCUPATION FOR THOSE WHO RUN OUT OF FUTURE"*

This sentence from an anonymous source says it all.

Realize that you may have been full of life and inspiration in your youth, but you haven't used all that verve to make your life easier.

You looked good, but you really unaware of it?

You had ideas that were generally not implemented by you.

Since you haven't always believed in yourself, you've missed out on tons of opportunities.

Remembering all these setbacks is bound to hurts.

It has been revealed in interviews that among retirees the explanation for "lack of energy" is primarily a mantra against new challenges.

It's a good reason to believe that in the midst of a gripping movie or TV series that you faithfully follow, it would be hard to move most of you out of your TV spot.

You would find yourself going through the illustrious catalogue of explanations for why you should not do it.

I am busy; I have no motivation; it is late and so on, becomes the reasons for your laziness.

If, however, you are informed late in the evening that you are flying into London for two nights, including a five-star hotel and a West End show, everything is prepaid and you are leaving in two hours.

Your deep love for the West End spectacle may make you forget your tiredness, lack of desire, etc., and you will certainly be ready within an hour at the airport.

But where and how did you mobilize the power and energy to accept this invitation? This is enough to inspire you.

Let's continue with the same pattern of thought:

It is in our hands and no matter how old we are; it is only a matter of decision which begins with the search for stimuli, to give us the right excitement, that we can use to transform negative energy into positive.

By the way, there are people who would reject a proposal like this and the question here is what will inspire them?

As our generation has changed a lot when it comes to meeting the challenges of old age, we need an alternative approach compared to previous generations.

> *Be Reminded That:*
> *Maturity is a state of mind. Age is just a number.*

CHAPTER FOUR

DAVID'S FAMILY SERVICES STORY

I am David, a retiree who recently celebrated 69 years of successful work and life.

Living after retirement can be difficult, with many entering their senior years unable to live the lives they thought they could, forcing retirees to face a whole host of new challenges that they are not able to cope with.

But my story is totally different, I was looking for work after I retired, but no one wanted to hire someone my age. I was already giving up after many attempts, until one day my neighbour, a single mom, wondered if I would be home for the next three hours, and if I could wait for the handyman who was supposed to fix the clogged faucet in her apartment building, otherwise she would have to wait for him and it will waste her whole day of work.

I immediately agreed. She left me the keys to her apartment, and the handyman arrived two hours later, fixed the clogged faucet and left.

She returned from her job at the end of the day, greeted me and demanded to compensate me for my support. I refused to accept anything from her on behalf of the good neighbours, but she insisted and didn't let go. She gave a speech that changed my life:

Agnes explained: "One of the typical phenomena of the 21st century among young couples is that both partners are active in their careers most of the day."

Many residences are structured so that at least 5 days a week and sometimes more, the wife and husband work very long hours. "There are single-parent families like me where the wife stays at work most of the day and there are lots of chores waiting for her when she gets home." They spend time and resources that after a day's work they do not have enough time for any other things. Couple of people are on a tight and exhausting schedule, and often they have to give up important tasks that need attention.

In the situation we have today, for example, continues Agnès, I called a handyman to fix the clogged faucet. I was told he would arrive in three hours, which meant I would spend a third of my productive day waiting for him and I'm not sure he would be here. Imagine, after waiting for three hours, and it takes another hour or two to repair the leak. I'm missing half a day's work in this situation. So, I'd better pay you for the support you provide to me.

Agnes continues: "My friend has to stay at home tomorrow, wait for a delivery. That is why she will not be able to go to work. If you are free tomorrow, you can wait for the package at her place, and she can go to work".

I realized at this point that there was a business opportunity here. A business concept that really didn't require money and a job that someone my age could easily do. All that is required is integrity to do this kind of work. After several weeks of doing various service assignments in my community for families, I recruited retirees to help me provide services in various areas.

I have 12 employees today, who provide different type of services, like taking the dogs out and walking them or taking them to a vet, escorting the children to school, watering the plants in the building, waiting for the professionals to receive from registered mail to home, transfer a vehicle license and a long list of regular jobs.

I am now a business owner that provides family services and helps keep other retirees involved by hiring them. I'm working now because I want to, but not because I have to. This is not the case for many elderly citizens today. After I started my business life wasn't the same.

DAVID'S TIPS

- "When you start a small business, you need to keep a close eye on prospects, they may appear from the market, services or new ideas,"
- "Your small business offers the opportunity to influence all parts of the system, allowing you to communicate your personal preferences while creating a rewarding and productive lifestyle."
- "Offer an ability to discover meaning and achieve goals that match your values,"
- "Serve as a motivation to get up every morning and an environment in which to function,"
- "Isolation could turn deadly as we grow older,"

Age as A Mental Limitation

In the previous chapter we discussed the fact that it's all in your head, we're going to discuss age as a mental limitation in this chapter.

Just imagine that you are twenty years younger than you think.

Consider a situation where you just received a letter from the Home Office, shortly after your retirement, telling you that they made a mistake on your date of birth and that you are 20 years younger than your actual age.

All of a sudden, you feel fresh, young, full of vitality and ready to pursue a new career?

Or maybe you are thinking of doing something else, something that you always wanted to do.

The reality is that due to a bureaucratic error, no one has ever become younger.

Your life expectancy would have averaged 40 to 45 years, 150 years ago, but now that health and medical treatments are improving, you can live your 80s, 90s and beyond.

If you ask scientists "what slows down aging?" you will get answers like eating healthy and eating less, exercising, controlling chronic stress, getting enough sleep.

Nevertheless, a lot of individuals do just that, but they still don't feel any younger.

The real question we should ask ourselves is what causes some people to enjoy excellent health and active lifestyles well beyond their traditional retirement age.

What is the X factor that makes us slow down our aging process?

Maybe people manage to slow down aging because they have decided not to get old at the expected rate.

People have been paying attention from the neck down, but probably, in reality, we have to pay attention from the neck up. It turns out that the story we tell about ourselves, to ourselves and the world, matters a whole lot. And even the way we think about aging itself, matters.

Faith, Belief and Intention are powerful forces in the process of aging

The new solution is to get yourself out of the middle-aged water that actually swallows you up to help improve your thinking.

So, to cultivate a young, creative and enjoyable approach to life, you need to stimulate yourself.

CHAPTER FIVE

ABOUT ELLEN LANGER'S YOUTH PRIMES

At Harvard, psychologist Professor Ellen Langer has spent nearly four decades researching what we know as "Youth Prime".

Anything that makes you feel young is prime.

And what Ellen found was that on a whole range of physiological tests, people exposed to youth bounties scored higher.

Their vision has improved; they have an improved hearing. Things such as grip strength and working memory also undergoes positive development.

The technique of this approach is for you to believe:

Look for a strategy to believe that you are smarter, sharper, and more involved than your birth certificate says, and your body will recalibrate itself if you ever find a way to accept those strategies. So, what you need to do is position yourself on the youth prime.

ELLEN LANGER AGE REVIEW EXPERIENCE

Since Langer couldn't actually send elderly people into the past, she decided to bring the past into the present.

In her 2009 book, "We would recreate the world of 1959 and ask subjects to live as if it were twenty years earlier," she writes, "counterclockwise."

How exactly did it work? Here's how Bruce Grierson in The New York Times Magazine presented the start of this experiment:

In their 70s, eight men climbed out of a van outside a converted monastery in New Hampshire.

They shuffled forward, a few of them arthritically stooped, a couple with canes.

And they walked through the door, entering a time warp.

On a vintage radio, Perry Como sang. On a black and white television, Ed Sullivan invited the visitors. It meant 1959 is a symbol to everything inside the house, including the books on the shelf and the magazines lying around.

These men didn't just know what things looked like back then; they were told to behave like it was 1959.

As if it were in the news, they dealt with historical events, and no arrangement was made to recall the fragile physical condition of these men; nobody held their bags, helped them up the stairs, or handled them like they were old.

"No mirrors, no contemporary clothes, no photos except photos of their much younger selves, nothing to spoil the illusion that they had shaken 22 years out of their age.

A week later, both the control group and the experimental group showed improvements in "physical strength, manual dexterity, gait, posture, perception, memory, cognition, taste sensitivity, hearing, and vision," Langer wrote in "Counterclockwise." Also, full 63% of them had better intelligence test scores at the end of the experiment than they did at the beginning.

In the experimental sample, four independent participants, who knew little about the research, looked at the before and after photos of men and saw the "after" photos as two years younger on average than the previous ones. "

Langer wrote on the last day of the study that "some men who, days before, had looked so fragile ended up playing an impromptu football game on the lawn."

Langer said the experimental subjects had "put their mind in an earlier time," and their bodies went along for the ride.

"If a number of older people can accomplish such a big change in their lives, we can too, and also, we have to ask ourselves if the limits we see does really exist ..."

ELLEN LANGER'S SUGGESTIONS

Beyond the practical steps outlined in the following lessons, if you are considering becoming an entrepreneur, the first and most important way to do it is to:
- Listen to yourself, your thoughts, your true desires.
- Dare to be more adventurous, experiment the thing that interest you.
- Live the life you want and dream of your own life, not the lives of others
- Stay busy, stay active
- The result of the thing you visualize is what should turn you on.
- Opportunities are fueling the new economy in the modern way of life, and today there are many. Their realization and use are the result of action and not of age.

"Don't stop dreaming about the things you want," *(Martin Luther King).*

CHAPTER SIX

MARCO'S PHOTOGRAPHY STORY

I am Marco, a former sales manager for a large company that supplies sporting goods.

Logic says we will all retire at some point in our lives. For others, retirement will follow an orderly progression and they will take the plunge at age 65 with sufficient pension funds. Others may be forced to adapt to the changing reality of difficult times and before they are ready to retire, they may find themselves out of work. And some people will move from one chosen profession to another, preferring not to withdraw from the world of work, but to remain active. No matter what path you find yourself on, it can be difficult to transition into retirement.

As for me, at 61, I was forced to retire because of the need to reduce company expenses. I had no idea what else to do with my life at the time. But I was an amateur photographer, just because I love taking pictures, and as a retirement gift I got a professional camera from my children and grandchildren.

I have always been passionate about photography, and it was a good time to express my creative spirit. I decided to take the subject seriously and signed up for a professional photography course. I studied different photographic techniques for four months. It's crucial for turning my hobby into a career. Studying for a technical certification has helped me gain the knowledge and skills necessary for me to thrive in the photography industry to. It gave me the ability to practically develop myself and gain invaluable knowledge of modern professional industry, which taught me how to best cope with it and forge a future for myself. I was able to strengthen my faith through the course and also learn more about my own strengths and limitations as a photographer.

I became busy with my two favourite activities at the end of the course: photography and exploring nature. As you know, I have time to explore.

I showed my photos of the landscapes I had to my friend, and they asked me to frame them, and they insisted on paying me for them. The growing desire for a business idea became what started out from a hobby.

The way to decide to turn a hobby into a business from here was short. I was motivated to start a business, rented a store that became a successful business hostel, strongly expressing my passion with the help of photographs, having participated in several successful exhibitions in which my photographs sold in record time.

The eyes of the world are the people who make up today's vibrant photographic culture, and I'm proud of it. We educate, encourage, amaze, and we place our world in the larger sense of history for people to see from a broader perspective, whether they are existing artists and journalists or new passionate voices.

But this photography group also faces major challenges with declining sales, fierce competition, and fragile confidence in the mission of educating photographers. Too often, these variables can cause us photographers and photo editors to lose sight of what drives us to preserve people's memories.

But now, at 65, I can look back on the four years I created and continue to have a profitable and rewarding business with satisfaction. Recently, I was asked to provide a large hotel chain with several hundred framed landscape photographs.

The common language of our time is that of images. Everyone has hundreds of them in their wallet, maybe thousands. They turn the scale, weightless, and the argument has always been what happened here? The images do not get old or distort. The strings of a brilliant photographer never go out of tune, which is why I could easily fit in at my age.

It is because of this that I am a photographer. We are the ones who sort through all the turmoil in the world and turn them into pictures that add meaning to a free life for all. We are the observers and the artists capable of distilling the confusion and the surrounding beauty in our world. We draw our attention to the things that you miss in your daily life, and we draw your attention to events and people that are far from your own universe. We know what we know differently and better when we focus our eyes and hearts with precision and sincerity. I have learned to look again and to look harder as a photographer. I take an image from several points of view.

For me, it started with this passion for photography and the desire for a tool that would put me in a position to engage with the world on a daily basis.

Retirement can be an opportunity for people, as I am currently pursuing mine, to finally make my dreams come true. It's a way for us to do things we've never had the time to do before. Because I see, I shoot. I shoot because I don't know who would if I don't.

MARCO'S TIP

- I have found that aligning values, harmony and balance between work, family and friends is the secret to a successful project.
- I feel like I'm the luckiest person in the world because I do what I really love, I get horny every day; I feel like anything is possible and I have the potential to get there. This dream has come true.

Reflection and Application: Your Personal choice And Priorities

I have a set of mental limitation questions framed for you to ask yourself here. These questions will test your mind and encourage you to acquire useful information. You should reach deeper within you to search and find answers to those unanswered questions.

The questions will help you understand what your personal choices and aspirations are and allow them to grow into a life that makes sense to you and is worth living every day.

Take the test now, and before continuing, spend 30 minutes answering it.

- What would you like?
- Where are you now?
- What is missing in your life?
- What does a precious life mean to you?
- What are the things that are really important to you?
- Why is this important to you?
- What are your priorities?
- How would you like to live?
- What one area would you like to change in your life?
- What would you really like to create in your life?
- What are these visions that you are forever putting on the back burner?
- What makes your heart skip a beat?
- What are your three greatest qualities?
- What are you most excited about now?
- What is one way to bring more energy into your life?

Take a notebook, scribble down your ideas and add your own useful questions

CHAPTER SEVEN

KAREN'S FRIENDLY FACE STORY

"Hello, my name is Karen. The worrying thing is that in silence, without communication and without friendly faces, a high percentage of seniors go through difficult and oppressive days with no one to speak or share their experiences and their opinions. My clients are a wide range of people of advanced age, not necessarily those in need of nursing or physical assistance, but people who want to meet other people,

I am 74 years old and this is my story. Eight years ago, while I was lounging in my neighbourhood cafe reading the newspaper, a widow in her eighties came up to me and introduced herself as Sarah, and asked if she didn't bother me because she needed to talk to me. I was amazed by the fact because it's not every day that someone comes up to you and asks that she wants to talk to you. I was intrigued, so I invited her over to my table.

Sarah began to express her take on the main newspaper article, and when she realized that my patience and time was at her discretion (still curious), she launched into a conversation where I politely nod and shows interest in the deeper reason for our seemingly arbitrary reunion.

About an hour later, as she is about to leave, Sarah asked me to allow her to pay for my coffee as a gesture and gratitude for the time I had given her, and asked me if she could meet me next week.

I accepted the offer, and it turns out that Sarah told me at our second meeting that there were several elderly people who are single for various purposes, have lost their friends, have no parents or are away from family or for other purposes.

Social isolation has to be the worst enemy of any individual, but it is a particular feeling for seniors. Sarah keeps telling me that there is no one to communicate and share with her a word, an experience or a childhood memory from the past, an attention or someone to spend time with him periodically at the cafe or the bistro. Here Sarah suggested that I serve as a companion once or twice a week, but not without payment.

How can I accept money from her seems surreal to me, but Sarah has successfully convinced me to accept his request and view it as a business proposition and as an investment that would benefit many people?

Since that conversation eight years ago, I have successfully started a business with Dana, my friend and my partner. Today, our company employs 40 seniors who provide emotional support and other services to single seniors.

We also hire ten young people who accompany our clients in all kinds of logistical and technical activities, such as filling in official paperwork, paying bills, simple home first aid repairs, reading and interpreting documents for those with reading or language problems.

Modern technology makes older people feel insecure and sometimes even threatened. Karen's partner Dana says it's natural to feel endangered by things you don't understand. "Our employees offer different levels of help and assistance to our consumers so that they can cope with the challenges that modern life presents to them." From the use of the smart cell phone, the remote control of the computer or the television, and of course, the resources of the companies from which they have developed other means of support. "

Since a large portion of the population is geared towards the elderly, there is immense potential for home care as the huge baby boomer generation enters their retirement years. Many older people tend to stay in their homes as long as possible, but as the pressures of old age set in, it becomes more and more difficult to do so without help.

By starting this business, we were able to help these people stay at home and spend their final years and decades with respect and dignity while creating a sustainable income for ourselves.

KAREN'S TIP

- The best approach we took was to "jump in and get started".
- "Positive responses from your friends and family will empower you and create a solid platform for your continued activity."
- "Trust what you do; your customers understand or appreciate what you have given them and you will gain their trust"

You Are Never Too Old to Be an Entrepreneur

We have discussed the mind set of people our age and mental limitation in previous chapter, in this chapter I want to discuss about the relationship between your age and entrepreneurship.

If you think you are too old to become a business owner, think again.

Many people in our culture think that establishing a new business is not for people over 60. This assumption is simply not valid.

The opposite is the case.

In fact, with many people enjoying good health and active lifestyles well beyond the conventional retirement age, becoming an entrepreneur after retirement is an increasingly common option.

Age shouldn't be a barrier to making a contribution to yourself, your family, and the community in which you live.

As we mentioned in previous chapter, "it's all in your mind," which means it all depends on the state of mind.

Let's take a look at this scenario regarding entrepreneurship, as regarding the topic of mindset

You are over 60 years old. Due to cuts in the industry in which you worked; you took an early retirement. A year has passed after leaving the company.

The whole subject of state of mind seems abstract, but you are depressed and living in fear, you have no control over your actions and thoughts.

An apt response:

It is very important that you apply your wishes, set your goals and strive to achieve your goals, but it is important not only to achieve your goals but also on method, desires and hope.

All of these considerations have an impact on your state of mind.

Realizing that you are at retirement age does not mean that you have to trust your family or the community in which you reside and be a burden. Equally important is the fact that you have to lean on your wits, your instincts, and not listen to those who tell you that you are too old to start an entrepreneurial career.

People don't know your deep feelings, your passions, and they don't know your dreams for sure.

> *Age is not an obstacle to creativity in business.*

In the decades to come, the decisions we made when we were young influence the course of our lives, but they do not oblige us and do not affect us at retirement age.

On the contrary, we have more freedom to choose whatever we want, without influences and considerations of external factors, at retirement age.

If we believe this, we can recognize that retirement is an opportunity, not a problem.

One would also think that the argument "life begins at sixty" is not a worn-out slogan.

The truth is, in your life, you can look for something that helps you feel younger for as long as possible.

Just because of a specific date in your calendar, it makes little sense to throw out all the knowledge and experience you've gained.

You can easily change careers with increasing life expectancy when you are 60, 70 or older and experience incredible entrepreneurial pleasure for years to come.

So, take control of your life and do something fun and fulfilling while improving your life and contributing to society at the same time.

Do not trap yourself in this boring retirement situation.

You Are Never Too Old To Be A Businessman.

The reasons below validate this reflection:

The desire to keep working, to be proactive and to get involved after 60 fosters a long-life expectancy and a balanced mindset.

You know what you are doing and what is your added value by the time you reach your age. This gives you the information you need as an entrepreneur to achieve your goals.

You know what excites and stimulate you. One of the perks of being at your current age is that you are done learning and is now playing with all of your choices.

In the morning, you know what is forcing you to get out of bed and go to work.

It's not just about learning to be motivated, it's also about feeling. This is what makes motivations so important; they make you feel that you are on the right track in life and give us confidence for a happy and exciting future.

You bring your expertise, your knowledge and your maturity in your chosen field, you have in-depth skills and training that you can use to make your business a success.

To get your business off the ground, you have the necessary resources.

You've built a vast network of useful contacts throughout your career and have the skills to form strategic partnerships to move your business forward, and you're probably excellent at building relationships.

You'll know when to surround yourself with the right people (sales manager, auditor, lawyer, and mentor) or learn new skills when you reach the age you are now (tech, social media)

These are all invaluable assets, and they are yours.

In addition to this, there are situations in which financial instability is typical of many people over 60 and increases the need to continue working beyond retirement age.

Discrimination on the basis of age leads to lack of advancement.

One alternative to existing work is entrepreneurship.

Let's focus on the benefits of entrepreneurship. Freedom and versatility. We want an adult to be his own boss.

The most popular reason you are likely to get when interviewing boomer entrepreneurs starting their business is to be their own boss and create a job that suits their lifestyle, with control of their hours.

Mature entrepreneurs, working on projects they love and following their interests and passions, are there for the love of what they do.

You need aspirations that give you hope and a reason for the future to continue living a full and positive life and doing something that you love, day in and day out.

Entrepreneurship is a source of energy that allows you to become more actively involved in your life instead of being a bystander and letting life move through you.

You are never too old to imagine this dream or set a goal for yourself.

You must refuse to spend your life in non-stimulating hobbies, the sole purpose of which is to pass the time, whether you are nearing retirement age or already retired.

A dream is not an illusion because you already know the distinction between dream and fantasy at your age, and your perspective is much more realistic.

You have the right and the independence to express and have your ideas respected.

Entrepreneurship will disrupt the routine; you will avoid living a monotonous life as society expects.

Entrepreneurship gives you the ability and the energy to expand your limits and increase the number of choices you have.

Schedule, vacations, and time management can be managed.

In some types of businesses, you can operate from home.

You get self-realization.

You benefit, directly or indirectly, from the future income you generate and also contribute to the community.

Entrepreneurship is a new status for people reaching their retirement years and an exceptional chance to have a refreshing life opportunity.

It will inspire you and lead to a new vocabulary about your place in modern society.

The response to the question I asked was How long will you continue to work. "As long as I can stand on my feet". The answer is strong and lasting.

At our generation, TIME is not a rare commodity, but it is up to you to make use of it favourably.

CHAPTER EIGHT

EVA'S BAGS AND BELTS DESIGN STORY

I'm EVA, and I am 69 years younger, and I want to tell that my best moment was when I was 12 years old when I discovered the creative part of me.

I sewed bags and belts from all manner of raw materials as a kid. I believed myself to be a creative person. In sixth grade, I remember my friend Naomi and I tried to convince neighbours and friends to purchase the belts and bags we made, and we didn't quite understand why they bought our beautiful products.

We set up a tent in the basement of our house, tried to incorporate our "products" into the spirit of the moment, replicated some samples from various fashionable magazines, but the sales were a disappointment. While other kids were building huts on trees, or building "Lego," models, we were busy creating bags.

I always knew that I had a creative spirit despite this unsuccessful experience, but unfortunately, until my retirement, I worked as a teacher most of my life.

We all have aspirations. It's easy to forget the inner voice of our brains as we beaver away in our professional jobs, caught up in the day-to-day rush. The dream we have, the one thing we would really love to do all but forgotten. I remember this phase in my childhood as the best time of my life, and I never left that vision of being a designer. Eventually, this vision has become a possibility.

It began three years ago, when I was sixty-six, I enrolled in a course in handbags and leather goods designing and manufacturing. I didn't hesitate when I learned about this course; I didn't consult anybody, I just signed up as though it hadn't been so many years since the experience of childhood. It was an inner voice I knew I had to accept.

The program took five months; good hands still serve me. Over the years, my artistic sense and imagination have never been harmed. In a trendy line and a mischievous wink for women of all ages, I began to design my collection of handbags and belts.

My competitive advantage was my concepts and high-quality raw materials, the start was slow, I worked from home, the costs were low, and I worked with different workshops that created my designs and I ended up with a complete collection after a short time. The primary cost was the raw material.

My vision and ambition have not been affected by the slow speed of sales; they were my engine to continue, they inspire me and lead me back to happier times. This was my second childhood.

Here is the twist in the story. I was invited to dinner with my good friend Naomi one day. She also invited David, her nephew from New York. Yes! the same Naomi who shared my store in the basement 55 years ago. David was the chief merchandiser of one of the United States' biggest retail chains.

She told David about my company before I reached Naomi, and the latter conducted the conversation so that I could tell him about my products. We agreed that I would bring him samples for analysis the next day, and David offered to show it to other buyers. We settled on the technical details and I have not stopped smiling since then.

Six months ago, a big corporation bought my business along with a bundle of shares for a handsome amount of money. They named me as the head of the department of design. I'm leaving the life that I dreamed in my baby hood now much better than I thought of it. Of course, it is much more satisfying and more enlightening to witness the pursuit of your dreams than the achievement of your dreams themselves. You now understand what the experience of childhood is.

EVA'S TIP

- In business terms, we must test any business decision. You'll be thrilled with your work if you're an artist, but if you want to turn your art into a successful business, you have to think about what the business needs. Your art is going to be part of your product's charm, but you have to realize that your product needs to be marketable.
- The fuel that drives successful business entrepreneurs is the confidence in the value of the organization and the determination to achieve the objectives.

Characteristics of The Older Entrepreneur

We will discuss the characteristics of the older entrepreneur in this section.

You must have asked yourself these questions at one time or another

Am I the right type of person to run my own business?

Do I have what it takes to become an entrepreneur?

You are going to have a pleasant surprise,

Entrepreneurship is not a quality you were born with.

Here are some facts about older entrepreneurs.

Due to the economic, human and social resources accumulated throughout their careers, older entrepreneurs are more likely to start and run a business than their younger counterparts.

In particular, research results indicate that the survival rates of businesses started by older entrepreneurs are higher than those of younger entrepreneurs.

Older entrepreneurs have a distinct leadership style.

Older entrepreneurs tend to be less concerned with improving their personal profile.

Older entrepreneurs don't need to prove their ability.

Without feeling intimidated by it, they consider the potential of others; they trust themselves.

They prefer to easily delegate responsibilities and create effective teams.

Older entrepreneurs are equipped with a range of connections that are not open to their younger counterparts.

They know who to turn to if they need to raise money, find investors, or enter new markets.

Be Optimistic

A mature entrepreneur always looks on the bright side.

He is looking for how he can really do things and make the world a better place.

He does not dwell on the past or on the unpleasant. He insists on going ahead instead.

The Perfect Entrepreneur

There is no such thing as the perfect entrepreneur, and there is no such thing as an entrepreneurial personality.

No matter what type of character you have, you can be successful.

Anyone can be a successful entrepreneur; they are all over the world.

And with your experience, I'm sure you can run your own business.

The value of a good work-life balance is understood by older entrepreneurs. They delegate easily, prefer shared responsibility over direct responsibility, and understand the challenges inherent in growing a business, especially when the economic climate is uncertain.

Because of their experience, knowledge, and the bumps and bruises that come with age, older entrepreneurs are said to have different attitudes towards business.

There is a wider and deeper network for older entrepreneurs which is an important part of doing business and also raising capital and other funding.

They have a greater sense of security without feeling threatened, so they can seek out the best candidates for their team.

Older entrepreneurs want to stay involved and engaged, but most importantly, they want to chart their course in a way that allows them to benefit from a corporate leadership experience.

Passion and inspiration are perhaps the two most critical characteristics for entrepreneurs.

Desire is crucial for the success of any business owner or professional. There would be no justification and no driving force for you to work without passion. Entrepreneurs love what they do and are incredibly committed to the businesses they create.

Motivation - Entrepreneurs are their own boss, which means no one is telling them to do something.

You need to be responsible for your own time and how you spend it.

Ask yourself the following questions to find out what your passions and motivations are.

1. Is there something I can work on over and over again without getting bored?

2. Is there something at night that keeps me awake because I haven't yet done it?

3. Is there something that I love doing so much that for the rest of my life I want to keep doing it?

Another important attribute of a senior entrepreneur is ethics.

Most entrepreneurs are responsible only for themselves and therefore need to have "a strong sense of basic ethics and integrity".

By doing business with an entrepreneur who lacks integrity, consumers and investors alike will lose interest.

It is important to note that research data indicates that there are a greater number of senior female entrepreneurs.

CHAPTER NINE

JACOB'S WEB CONTENT WRITING TALE

My name is Jacob and for over two years I have been writing content for various corporate websites.

According to the standards and specifications of search engines that adjust and update themselves from time to time, the Internet environment is constantly based on quality content and the right channels for which it is intended.

The content of a website today, more than ever, needs to be insightful, compelling, authentic and welcoming to readers and inspire them to take action.

At the same time, by using keywords and phrases that will maximize the web's rating, the content must convey a delicate balance.

There is no company, organization or private person today that does not understand the need for a site to support its business interests and also act as a marketing tool.

A website for online selling, or placement, branding and recognition, and as a digital business card, should be accessible to those who want to showcase, sell or provide their products or services.

There are several courses that provide you with theoretical knowledge about writing materials and practical experience.

My grandson told me two years ago, on my 68th birthday, that his friend had set up a course on writing content for websites and because he knew that one of my favourite hobby was writing. As a birthday present, he signed me up for the course.

The course gave me technical aspects, practical experience and tools to help me use my writing skills to write content according to the product and target audience suitable for the internet.

In order to transform what I love to do into a career, I had to Study for a professional qualification. This has helped me develop the knowledge and skills to excel in the industry. It gave me the opportunity to improve my writing skills and gain invaluable knowledge of modern professional industry, which taught me how to best cope and build a career as a writer.

What really moves me is the concern for what I want, the opportunity to write at my age, it's never too late to use our imaginations as a source of income and work with influential people.

I established a large client base in a relatively short time, expanded my website writing and newsletter writing business, and trained four retired teachers.

I agreed that each of the writers would specialize in a specific industry in order to have a quality and competent writing service. Each staff member works from home and we come together to collaborate and share experiences once a week in the neighbourhood café.

I don't plan on quitting anytime soon. I have the dream of widening the circle of writers and of training other writers.

"As long as I remember my name and address, I will continue," Jacob said in a simple and cheerful manner.

JACOB'S TIP

- A specialization in a particular field would allow you to be competent and knowledgeable in that particular field. There will be better quality in the work. You will save time

because you will have enough experience to find these details, the service will be better, and you can reduce the costs. In a given sector, you can stand out and build a reputation.
- The demand for outsourced service providers is increasing every year due to productivity, flexibility and above all service costs. As a result, several possibilities have been developed for business service providers. The advantage is that you can operate from anywhere from your home, neighborhood cafe, or the beach using technologies like email, internet, and Skype. All you need is a good marketing plan, a phone, a computer, and an Internet connection to be successful.

Change your Perspective

It is important to understand the mental processes that produce our thought patterns, our understanding of events and circumstances, and our responses to them before moving on to the next chapter.

Perspective is a way of interpreting or looking at a certain event.

It is an attitude or a point of view about how something is perceived or thought.

Your perspective ultimately defines the experience of life, not the circumstances.

Not by changing all the circumstances, but by changing your perspective, you can change your life.

The reason I have added this section to this book is that people are sometimes trapped by perspectives and belief systems at any age, but especially our age, which they believe to be a specific part of them that can never be changed.

It can't be far from the truth if you are willing to change and at least look at other and different perspectives.

Limited perspectives keep us from getting what we want.

No matter how hard we try, they keep us from having different results.

Presumably only a few of our generation are aware of the tremendous effect on the way our outlook has on our lives.

Limited perspectives keep us from getting what we want.

The memories and experiences that have accumulated in our lives since the day we were born are the factors that shape our views.

Environmental factors such as the education we have received, social factors, faith, and all kinds of other factors that establish a pattern of thinking, perspectives, and perception of reality.

In order to determine which, one is the most appropriate, it is important to look at and analyse a specific situation from different points of view.

From a very subjective perspective that seems real and concrete, we are still "stuck" but in fact it is only a distortion of our reality.

Interpreting this fact tends to hamper our progress and prevent goals, including those we set for ourselves, from being achieved.

Looking at a narrow point of view not only prevents or hinders the accomplishment of an outcome, what we have achieved is often not the same or different from what we expected from the start, and this is unrelated with the effort that we have spent.

The truth of our lives is the meaning we give most of the time to the situations and circumstances around us.

In other words, we cannot refer to reality as it is, but to our perception of the same reality through our lens.

Stand up and think:

We can't change the circumstances in most cases, but we can certainly change our perspective and our decisions.

Find out about you:

What is my perspective of this subject which gives me this result?

What perspective could I take now that might help me resolve it?

In reality, we have to analyse situations from several points of view, given our experience.

Many individuals our age, however, tend to continue to live comfortable lives with a narrow point of view while ignoring the risks of living in such a position and ignoring that this area narrows over time and that the point of view becomes limited.

This scenario weighs heavily on our judgment for a different scenario or outcome.

Therefore, we prefer to adjust from a different perspective to automatic reactions to anything that shakes up our routine, without stopping for a moment to reflect and consider the occurrence and only then respond.

In our cramped comfort zone, we close ourselves off, avoid breaking it, and dare to visit a new and more intriguing place.

Perhaps we are not aware that from another point of view, that is deeper and clearer, we will see and experience circumstances much better. It is from another perspective that will open a window to a new experience of generating different perspectives. And who knows you can enjoy the process too.

Your ability to doubt the point of view will reveal and create various points of view and new ideas. When that happens, we call it Reframing. The ability to discern a point of view, at any time, is a powerful weapon.

Reframing is not about changing your mind. Rather it will help you see things in a whole new way, it's about creating a shift in consciousness. This change allows you to take a look at something from a whole new point of view or point of view.

Reflection And Application: Change Your Perspective

For what they are and what results they get, this task will uncover your old perspectives. Furthermore, this task will also show how daunting viewpoints can be and, alternatively, how new viewpoints make a life of empowerment and hope easily accessible.

Critical thinking can reveal old perspectives on what they are and the results they generate.

The following questions will reveal how new perspectives make a life of empowerment and hope available.

Additionally, the answers to these questions can identify restrictive viewpoints and old belief systems that highlight thinking that need to be changed if you really want different results.

Perspective question

- How perfect is the current situation?
- How could the current situation not be perfect?
- What doesn't make you change your situation?
- What will help you change your situation
- What would you do to produce a different result?
- What scenario would you like to be in?
- Describe one way that you could have made your life more enjoyable.
- If asked, what advice would you give to someone in your situation?
- How, instead of managing the situation, could you challenge the situation?
- Complete the sentence: "I cannot ...... because I ....".

Take a notebook, scribble down your ideas and add your own useful questions

CHAPTER TEN

BETTY'S SPECIAL COFFEE STORY

People love coffee, I believe so do you! Thanks to the great coffee giants, espresso drinks are more popular than ever. With so many coffee bars, it will be normal that many people want to start their own café. But when we think about starting this type of business, most people still focus on the social or enjoyable aspects of the business, which is natural.

But that's all they do sometimes. Some future coffee business owners, like my grandson, often jump in for the challenge of successfully starting and running a coffee shop. A cafe owner can quickly feel overwhelmed without asking tough questions about the key aspects of running a business. The result can contribute to burnout and business failure.

I am Betty; I am retired after 35 years of working as a consultant for a large company. I assumed it was time after several years of work to finally rest. Until one day my grandson came over in a foul mood and asked to tell me about his coffee, entrepreneurship business.

I asked him what had happened. I know he bought a cafe a year ago, and so far, he had said nothing about it. So, I assumed the business was doing well.

It wasn't exactly the case. From what he said, the business was taking losses. He couldn't keep up with the bank's loan repayments. He felt he was drowning, and he needed my advice to take the next step. I couldn't help but come to his aid. From the day it opened until the day my grandson decided to ask my opinion, it was the first time I heard about the business in detail.

So, I went to see my grandson again and after reviewing all the books fully, I discovered that it was important to change the whole model and the strategy of the coffee shop. "A good business is one that sells a product that references a specialty and sets itself apart from the rest of the competition." And since the coffee shop is located in a small neighbourhood and focused on frequent customers, it needs to be redefined to validate the tastes of customers and adjust its features accordingly. Since most of the locals in the neighbourhood are adults and there is also a senior citizens' home within walking distance of the coffee shop, I suggested that he designate the coffee shop operations to the adult audience.

It is a systemic transition involving several elements, such as access to strollers, more practical seats, fun background music, even classical music, a thoughtful menu alongside a standard menu and a culinary match for any age and palate. I also suggested that he make a list of the characteristics and habits of his potential customers.

I had no idea at the time that my grandson was hoping to hire me as a business partner. It was far from everything I expected for the future.

I am now happy to own a business in partnership with my grandson after many years of working for people and without any previous plans of owning or partnering in a business.

I recognize today that by being close to the age of my client, I am an additional asset for the company. Frequent patrons of the coffee shop now feel like they're in a special club. A Day in the Life of a cafe owner can be filled with endless juggling, delegation, and sometimes not enough time to complete anything, despite glimpses of meeting new people, and laughing with customers.

We have two branches in neighbouring towns four years after I joined the business, and we plan to sell franchises all over the world. I never thought about being the best when it comes to retirement age, nor did I expect me to run a business happily.

BETTY'S TIP

- Prepare a complete business plan with your passion and enthusiasm, as well as the support of your family.
- A guarantee of your success is your ability to distinguish your product from other competitors.
- Don't forget to have fun. One of the reasons you start your own business is enjoying life.
- You have to analyze them from several angles when you select and create new ideas. How you see the definition and how your target consumer sees the same idea makes a big difference.

When Work Turns into Game

The purpose of this chapter is to provide you with resources that will help you solve the challenges in your business and your life as a whole.

One of the rules of the business is to imitate the ones you see in games.

In the way you manage and run your business, you have to apply what you have learned - you will be more effective this way.

We should remember that any business is followed by a difficult period, despite all the advantages listed in third generation entrepreneurship.

Specific and complex problems are often difficult to solve in any business.

We have had good times and bad at our age, times of happiness and disappointments, crisis and solved problems.

We have come to a time where we want peace of mind, to enjoy spending time with our friends and family and enjoying our work more than anything else.

So, the question is, can we still enjoy working in the midst of the challenges and obstacles that affect our mood?

How do you navigate between obligations for the sustainability of a healthy lifestyle?

Why are we really so serious about our work?

If we look at the factors that influence our job to achieve a certain degree of satisfaction or the factors that affect our mood when facing a complex business problem, we find that the root cause is that we take the job too seriously.

As we get older, our approach to work changes and takes on a different meaning, but it does not always need to be serious.

The fear of failure is the explanation.

"FAILURE IS A DETOUR, NOT A DEAD STREET" (Zig Ziglar)

We are terrified of failure.

In all the institutions and societies that were responsible for our education and shaped our patterns of behaviour, they ingrained this feeling in us.

They taught us from our early childhood that winning is a good thing and losing is a bad thing.

Is it true? Not always, however! Instead of a scar reminding us of the mistakes we made, we see failure as a death blow.

We live timidly and are reluctant to take risks and try new starts.

The fear of failure becomes overwhelming.

In games, that doesn't happen.

When they fail in a match, players rarely give up or lose motivation

Instead, before trying the same situation again, they man up and learn from their failures.

A change in your understanding and attitude towards work begins with the prescribed way of obtaining job satisfaction.

You won't waste time and energy on regrets if you see work as some kind of game or even an adventure, just draw your conclusions and move on.

You will feel more efficient and there is a chance that you may even enjoy it.

There is no doubt that you will be faced with difficult business times at one time or another and that you will be able to resolve them, just as you do in your personal life.

Think of it as part of a game and ask yourself this question,

What's The Worst Thing That Can Happen?

When you know what it is, you can deal with the situation while creating something different with the understanding that it is only part of the game.

Your state of mind and understanding of the situation as a game frees you from pressures and concerns and makes challenges easier to overcome.

You really look at the case from a new point of view and get a different meaning when you take this approach.

Another way to overcome obstacles that may arise:

Imagine you are in a role-playing game with different characters in which you are having virtual conversation.

You can decide to think like Bill Gates, or Steve Jobs, or Mickey Mouse, or even like your mother-in-law, for example, think like someone else, how would they see and interpret the situation?

What will they do in the same situation? Imagine their responses to the situation?

From a number of perspectives, examine their reactions and attitudes.

This game will broaden the view and help establish a new and different perspective.

Choose a range of characters; know that for additional and enriching perspectives, they will open a new window.

Ask the person closest to you, ask yourself if these do not convey thoughts, ideas or solutions to the problems or dilemmas you are facing.

Another strategy that can help you cope with difficult business circumstances is to ask yourself insightful questions that can lead you to pleasantly improve your perspective.

How can you make the situation light?

Can you look at it with a different perspective?

You are Captain Kirk, as in the "STAR TREK" series. You are in a place where you have never set foot, what would you do in this place if you could?

What's the funniest thing you can get out of this position?

Your business game determines your own story and decides which direction you will take.

In your own story, you are the main character; how much you develop is up to you. "I AM THE MASTER OF MY FATE; I AM THE CAPTAIN OF MY SOUL" (William Ernest Henley)

It is only because it excites us and continues to be a new experience that a game remains enjoyable.

We need to have a plan for our business, a plan that will make us to be dedicated and deeply interested in what we are doing.

START YOUR OWN QUEST.

- Take the road less traveled. Without fear of the consequences, explore and experience.
- Do what have never being done before.
- On your own terms, run your business.
- Above all, don't forget to enjoy the game.

CHAPTER ELEVEN

RACHEL'S OUTSOURCING OFFICE SERVICES STORY

Outsourcing services occupy a prominent role in start-up companies, independent businesses, and small businesses. Office services are numerous and varied in the modern era, such as receiving messages and setting appointments, handling e-mails, accepting customer orders, maintaining offices, drafting mailings, getting ready various reports, managing blogs, preparing presentations and managing different processes and reports. The variety is broad and rich; you can specialize and focus on delivering one or more services in accordance with the preferences and training you want to bring to this business world.

My name is Rachel, and I retired at 64 after 37 years of civil service. I had already decided to start a company that offers office services to other companies during my last year of employment.

After my son opened an office building cleaning business and asked me to assist him with various office jobs, I came up with this business concept. There is a connection between the services rendered to the offices, as well as the cleaning of the office in my opinion.

What started out as a one-home service provider partnering with my son has grown into multiple businesses that meet the need of other business looking to outsource in a specific niche. We were able to start a small business that serves large companies, regardless of what they are into when they are looking to cut costs.

They are looking for the cheapest way to keep their business running smoothly. They prefer outsourcing rather than paying high wages and benefits to recruit workers for their business. They prefer to think of big companies that export to other countries when people think of outsourcing. Small businesses often outsource around the corner to small businesses.

All we had to do was make the appropriate services available upon their request. We device a way to provide large companies with the required service at a lower cost and give high quality service than what they could get from their own workers.

It's not just families who are outsourcing their "boring jobs". Small businesses can pay for quality cleaning services too! And that's where we come in. Accuracy of information is the secret to success in this business. We can provide the reliability and speed with each solution.

RACHEL'S TIP

- While there is a lot of competition due to a large number of companies offering office services, it will give you an edge over your competition if you focus on services in a certain industry in a certain area.
- Create consistency and an irreproachable level of work, and developing a reputation for an entity capable of meeting deadlines and assignments is most critical.
- Entrepreneurship is like a game; you challenge yourself, make plans, and invent new concepts.

Type Of Business For The Third Age

People keep asking themselves what is the best and most suitable business for senior entrepreneurs; my answer is that the best business is a business where you can excel in achieving your goals and improving your life.

Fortunately, there are multiple possibilities for us in old age to make different business choices, which make our business selection method very versatile.

In this chapter, I aim to illustrate some of the appropriate business opportunities for seniors in terms of the potential for effortless income generation and low-risk businesses.

You all must know the story of Mozart, who played violin and harpsichord at the age of 3 and composed small pieces of music at the age of 5 and write them with the help from his father. At the age of 6, he played the piano while covering his eyes. The role and future of the gifted child was transparent and secure.

Unfortunately, the future and the profession were not so obvious at our young age for most of us; our careers and our jobs have always resulted from circumstances.

We made critical decisions in our youth that were based on minimal knowledge with no real-life experience

These decisions were largely the product of external factors, such as parental power, education, environment and media.

It takes a long time to grow and realize and appreciate what we really want to be a part of, and suddenly we find ourselves in a mature era, and behind us a profession that we would not have chosen today.

What is really fascinating is how some people who feel like they are living their life in harmony with their life challenge or life purpose get there?

It is quite difficult not to be envious of people who understand this very early on.

Some people already know by the age of five that they want to someday be a world-class surgeon with no family history of surgeons.

THE MATURE ENTREPRENEUR

They dedicate their lives to this. They become this world-famous surgeon and are so thrilled and just feel like there is a significant contribution to their life. They love what they are doing. But the truth is, most of us are not like that.

The decision to start a business at our age, on the other hand, is a reasonable choice that is taken without pressure. It focuses on cumulative information, first about ourselves, about leadership style, and then about the business climate.

Now follow the instructions in the next exercise and your perfect business will magically unfold.

Right now, I want you to take the time to list the things that give you the greatest joy. It doesn't matter if you don't see them in your life right now. You just want to bring them to life. I'll also warn you to get them out pretty quickly. Don't try to become part of those that culture would mark as being with no desire and no energy as a senior.

And now make another list of those things you can do, even if you didn't pay to do them, things that you feel that time stops when you do them.

Once you've figured out the things you would do if you had nothing to hold back, go back and divide the list into categories that you would find more convenient to perform.

Note that it was not mentioned that you can absolutely delete them. Instead of going back and discussing your ideas, you want to try to organize them into different parts.

For example, you don't have a single thing like volunteering, sitting on the same roster as the NBA basketball player, that way. Exclude the impossible things from the list, like becoming an NBA basketball player.

Combine these two lists now, so that you have one master list. Give yourself permission to explore these elements, write on each element how you can incorporate them as you expand your thoughts about them, give them existence, and make them as visual as possible in your business mind.

How do you feel about your life starting your new business and going through these things?

Decades of business consulting have taught me that you must have the right mindset and the right behaviour combining it with optimism to be a great entrepreneur.

Know where you are and where you are going, accurately describing your personal and professional priorities.

When you start a business, you have one enormous advantage that separates you from the rest: the advantage of age.

A balanced look, from the point of view of your age and experience, is of great importance. What you have learned in your professional and personal life, and you are considering starting your own business using this experience.

Do this based on the list of criteria in front of you; the recommended considerations for reviewing a business for your age are:

- A business whose career represents your passion. It must include something that you have long wanted to do that would express your personal interests and desires. Out of fear, many of us have rejected our passion, believing that our passion is a dream that cannot be realized. We missed opportunities, but we can clearly see what are our needs today.
- A business that takes little time to set up and you will be involved in for the next 10 or 20 years.
- A business with the least possible risk.
- A business that can express and use your expertise, your experience, and your friendship must also come in handy. Personal relationships are essential for understanding and

taking advantage of opportunities. Maybe your business will grow out of them.
- A business that allows you to control all aspect of your work in order to share your values and build a happy and profitable lifestyle.
- A business that helps you to be versatile during working hours, to maintain a healthy lifestyle in which, when you want, you can achieve your desires.
- A business that attracts and excites you is both fun and satisfying.
- A business that you can also manage from home (if possible).
- A business that matches your capabilities, except taking a course or workshop to supplement the information, which does not require long and expensive research.

Most important, like Frank Sinatra Sung

"I DID IT MY WAY,"

A business founded on your own initiative will fascinate and challenge you, the company is controlled by you and it operates under your conditions and through you.

Reflection and Application: Find Out What Type of Business Is Right for You

A. Create a list of the ten most important things in your business and in your life that are important to you. Dream about how to make it fun to get them.

B. The following questions are intended to provide the entrepreneur with the direction you are looking for.
- Who would you like to be?

- If there was one thing you could do, what would be your dream business?
- What skills and competencies do you have?
- What are your main achievements?
- What are you doing so well?
- What do you like to do?
- What are your talents and skills?
- What would you like about the job?
- What will you need from the job?
- What interests do you have?
- What do you think you would like to do?
- What does your heart say?

Take a notebook, scribble down your ideas and add your own useful questions

CHAPTER TWELVE

LISA'S PERSONAL CHEF STORY

Hi, I'm Lisa by name and I'm a personal chef.

There is a great chance that you will become a good personal chef if you cook for the love of the culinary world, and are complimented by what your hands and talents do.

On special occasions and in small circles, corporate or seasonal meals, the personal chef prepares meals for individuals and families. These will generally be occasional events, and the cooking is done in the customer's kitchen.

Many chefs choose to be personal chefs because on their own terms they can develop a culinary career, let their imaginations run wild, and enjoy a schedule that they set. Such flexibility cannot be appreciated by a chef in a restaurant.

I decided to start my new career and develop a personal chef services business at the age of 65 with the help of my husband and family. I cleaned the necessary equipment and took a path that seemed promising to me.

A client who purchases the services of a personal chef expects a culinary experience that matches their tastes and desires. I felt secure to take on the new challenge without fear when I started my business. But I found out along the way that the reality was not how I expected things to turn out in other directions, and I realized I was wrong.

I learned that I was more interested in finding clients than improving my culinary skills and researching current trends.

"With a mixture of disappointment and confusion, I remember this time because everyone enjoyed what I was cooking, but not everyone was my customer. My husband and I tried, unfortunately without success, to sell our services as a personal chef as we knew.

I blamed everyone for my personal failure, I blamed customers, competitors, the business climate, and the world at large. I was ready to give up my dream and close the business, which was the most obvious conclusion at the time. I expressed my grief with my best friend and told her that I wanted to close my business, but she asked me to postpone my decision before meeting with a business coach.

I knew from our first meeting that giving up on the dream of a personal chef was a mistake, and my coach was there to keep me focused. Thanks to him, I learned that development can be part of distress and mistakes. He taught me how not to focus on yesterday's weaknesses and to streamline my energies to do now and tomorrow.

Because of the need for healthy foods, one of my coach proposals was to specialize in cooking for sick people. Diabetic foods, heart patients and diets suitable for people allergic to a particular form of food. I was intrigued by the concept. The action plan began with the process of learning about different forms of diet. I read and researched relevant research, interviewed doctors, nurses, and clinicians.

Now I have recently expanded and also run workshops besides cooking that deal with "cooking for special needs". I have three assistants today and have started writing a cookbook in my area of expertise.

LISA'S TIP

- Use a mentor or coach. Many people find it difficult to start a business because they don't have the resources to handle the many elements of starting a business. There are possibilities of failure without prior advice. For savings or other reasons, the temptation to do it alone in the world is a great temptation, especially for entrepreneurs who are just starting out. It can be a pit of death and a ray of hope. "Cooking a business is not like cooking food."

Debunking Myths About Third Age Businesses

In this chapter I would like to challenge some common misconceptions about entrepreneurship in general and in particular about becoming an older entrepreneur.

Myths largely reflect a natural or social phenomenon and often a common but false belief or principle.

"TIME IS MONEY" is the first myth.

When it comes to becoming an entrepreneur, the misconception that "time is money" still raises grave concerns.

The assumption that older people do not have time on their side is incorrect.

There has been an understanding of the need to balance work and leisure in recent years. For us at our age, "time is life" instead of time is money, and life is the balance between family, friends and leisure time at work.

"BUSINESS ENTREPRENEURSHIP HAS HIGH FINANCIAL RISK," is the next misconception

This misconception is also not true in itself; one of the goals of this book is to give you a unique perspective on the possibilities of starting an independent business with very low risk and with very little financial investment.

The success stories presented in this book are compelling evidence that it is possible to start a business with low financial risk after retirement.

> "A BUSINESS ENTREPRENEUR IS A GAMBLER," is the next myth:

This myth, like any other, has little basis at the age when you want to protect and manage the affairs of your life. When gambling is involved, it means that you cannot control the potential outcome in play?

Gambling and taking control over expected results are opposites and cannot occur at our age in the entrepreneurial definition. So, after retirement, losing control is not an option in entrepreneurship.

> "YOUNG ENTREPRENEURS ARE MORE SUCCESSFUL THAN OLDER ENTREPRENEURS"

In this myth, I see no reasoning. Our physical health is not something we can be proud of at our age, but what about our abilities, experience, personal and business relationships? After all the mistakes we have made, and after the failures and achievements we endured has led us to gain greater ability and invaluable experience.

There is still a long way to go for young entrepreneurs.

> *Another myth is: "ENTREPRENEURSHIP NEEDS BIG AND INNOVATIVE IDEAS,"*

Reality reveals that most entrepreneurial launches come from tiny innovations or the development of existing ideas. Between the invention of the wheel and the technical revolution, the possibilities for action of the initiators have always been and will be forever exploited.

> *The next misconception is: "RETIREMENT IS GOOD FOR SENIORS,"*

You will lose vitality in retirement, so you should accept that old age is not a retirement age, but a time and a life of fulfilment.

Take advantage of your age, as advanced as you are, to change your perception of retirement and make it another stage in your life.

The new recognition and change in perception around this time, like the leisure time combined with productive activity is gratifying.

> *And the last misconception is: "START A BUSINESS ONLY WHEN THE ECONOMY IS GROWING,"*

This is not entirely true, there are advantages to starting a low-risk business in times of economic uncertainty:

- Less rivalry
- Low risk businesses will thrive and even grow if inefficient businesses fail.
- You are expected to manufacture a product or provide quality services during the economic recession. You also

don't have the opportunity or the prospect to test the quality of your products or services in robust economies.

In their position as key chapters of history, it is necessary to get out of the myths. Although it is easier to establish legacies and acts of heroism and completely forget about myths when we are engaged in entrepreneurship.

CHAPTER THIRTEEN

ELSA EBAY SALES STORY

Hello, my name is Elsa, and this is my story of how after my retirement I built a successful business.

eBay is the Internet's largest and most popular shopping site. The site is essentially a global platform that enables local and international online commerce. The site provides private retailers and small businesses with a vast array of different items that power millions of users need every day, allowing their customers to open a personal online store.

eBay is a great forum for various sales opportunities due to the large number of visitors, so many users take advantage of this platform to conduct income-generating activities or even replace existing sources of income.

In October 2015, I started trading on eBay. I joined the Internet discussion group in which thousands of retirees from around the world participated. I met Peter and Eve who said they have an active eBay store which they described as a store that generates orders from all over the world and does not require a large investment in marketing and sales budgets. They said they woke up every morning rejoicing in the work of their hand.

In fact, it's not the first time I've learned about eBay. Sometimes I hear my grandchildren talking about the sales that occurs on the site, and even my son brought me a scarf for my 64th birthday the site.

Have you ever jumped into something you didn't even expect to do, but remember that you are well suited to do? And not only that, but you have a painful passion to do it all of a sudden? This is what I would call chasing dreams that you never really thought about.

Peter and Eve volunteered to lead attendees through the simple steps required to set up the store and operate on the web. I wanted to try my luck by selling four things that I made for fun and also out of curiosity: two scarves and two shawls that I knitted. To my surprise, someone bought my scarves and shawls. And I went from there to setting up the store with this idea.

The path was short, and I told my friends that I was looking to buy some hand-knitted items. My husband believed in the technological duties of photographing and uploading the items to the website, so I became the owner of a virtual store. Over time, this simple business grew stronger and helped improve our quality of life.

The e-commerce revolution is taking a leading role in the markets of the Western world, and this global stage has become an open market, that many retirees should stop being an audience.

eBay and Amazon are the pioneers of these trading platforms and there is also a good training offer for their establishment as there is a growing demand for virtual stores. Online store platforms are a very effective tool and solution for targeting a large global shopping audience and with relatively little investment. Life for me and my husband is very busy. We have time to travel and have fun with our family while we run our business.

ELSA TIP

- The success of an online store depends on many factors:
- Find what you like to sell.
- Find out what your customers think about your products.
- The cost of starting your own business has dropped dramatically in the 21st century. The internet and modern

technology allow you to sell anything, anywhere, to anyone.

Risks and Your Money

What are the risks involved in being an entrepreneur?

In a report on older entrepreneurs, the inability to take risks to start a new business was the most common explanation for avoiding entrepreneurship.

Many people tend to equate risk with entrepreneurship.

There are undoubtedly many individuals who, for fear of failure, prefer not to start a small business or develop their concept.

That doesn't mean you have to take any risks when it comes to readiness to take risks. To be successful as a business owner, you must select these risks you are taking and avoid the others, that the risk level is high.

When you have decided to start a business or have found a business opportunity, before deciding to move forward, weigh the challenges and the prospects, as well as the potential implications, positive and negative.

Measuring Risks involve

Starting a business involves small and large details, as well as facets of your life.

The approach does not differ from the way you calculate the risks in your life when it comes with your decision making. Just like without a thorough price estimate or taking into account your financial constraints, you wouldn't buy a house or a car, so would you start a business.

There are two major criteria to assess risk at our age, the psychological aspect and the financial aspect.

The first is the key that opens or delays a decision.

The second, more realistic and reasonable, takes into account and discusses the danger or opportunity involved in choosing, compromising or preventing the loss of assets or pension funds.

These two elements create a loop of indecision, which depends mainly on the psychological obstacle to be overcome.

Third generation entrepreneurs are more vigilant. Young entrepreneurs take financial risks faster, assuming they still have several years to cover their losses and assets.

With the rational hope that he has no "years to make up the investment." the entrepreneur of our age must be more vigilant and minimize financial risks.

This is reason enough for you to doubt the establishment of a business.

Not using retirement funds or losing investments and starting a business that doesn't need a big investment is one way to solve the risks.

I am sure you will agree that no one wants to sacrifice funds accumulated in a career for a future that is less than the past in the number of productive years we have to exploit and live, and therefore every entrepreneur must first identify the risks involved in setting up and operating the business.

A detailed plan should then be prepared and formulated to define how to identify and reduce the risks, starting with building a business plan.

Your money

The question of our attitude towards money and to what extent it determines the course of our life is more important than the amount of money we have in the bank.

"Money" is not, God forbid, a negative term, since we all aspire to economic freedom. But from an appropriate and critical point of view, we must consider it.

Despite the acceptance of greed as an important economic driver, at a certain age its influence on us as individuals can upset the balance in our life.

The purpose of money must be a means and not an objective.

Money carries emotional baggage and becomes the centre of our fears, sets the limits of our success and tests our self-esteem.

So, you need to disconnect (as much as possible) the relationship between your emotions and your bank account balance as an important business consideration. The typical roles of a regulated executive would be reversed in this way.

It is to regulate and deprive the money of its control over you. Money is your accessory and not the opposite.

As you look back on your life and assess what caused problems and failures in your life, you may find that money is not the main reason for this, so you have to remember that in the future, the same money will not solve all your problems.

There are advantages to not having money in your business. In the generation and development of solutions, the lack of an adequate source of funding produces processes of ingenuity and innovation.

In your inventiveness and distress, your ingenuity will be reflected, a chain of financial strategies will be brought down, your view of the true nature of challenges and inhibitions will be altered, and a window of adaptation from a position of experience and knowledge of life will open.

Lack of financial investment will test your entrepreneurial spirit in a new and adapted reality of creative marketing thinking. Lack of money is the stimulus that will make you aware of the possibilities of saving money or raising low risk sources of finance.

Luck

Entrepreneurs usually ask if they need to be lucky to be successful in business. let's first describe luck.

The description of luck in Merriam Webster's dictionary is:

1. A force that brings wealth or adversity to good.
2. The circumstances or conditions that work for or against a person.

> *The Roman philosopher Seneca said:*
> "luck is what happens when preparation meets opportunity"

Luck would do so under predetermined conditions of professionalism and manipulation of possibilities, if it wishes to appear.

In order to give yourself a gift, the absence of these requirements is like a closed door that someone tries to enter.

For your chances of success, don't look at the luck statistics; you must build your business on realistic, sustainable and achievable behaviour. All must achieve a dosage and consistency greater than the values, luck and hope that you are committing to.

It is important that when the opportunity arises, businesses are ready.

While there can be a lot of luck in the essence of timing, the ones that are capable of it are the companies that will take advantage of the opportunities. Most of what happens in business is that chances are not lost because business is bad, but because it is not prepared.

Gary Player, the South African golfer, once said:

THE HARDEST I DRIVE, THE LUCKIER I GET

Likewise, Thomas Jefferson wrote that,

THE MATURE ENTREPRENEUR

"I HAVE A GREAT BELIEF IN LUCK, AND I FIND THE HARDER I WORK, THE MORE I HAVE OF IT,"

What Jefferson was getting at was that luck and our ability to use luck to work for us is neither natural nor indiscriminate; it is the product of hard work, actions and attitudes.

To find out how essential they think a little luck is in business, I spoke to some successful entrepreneurs.

They respond that in some cases chance will play a role. Sometimes you just find yourself in the right place at the right time, and it feels like a lucky break. But it's the hard work, drive, commitment and unconditional trust in your concept that will take you forward from their experience.

Of course, luck plays a role in success, being in the right place at the right time certainly helps with the right product, but you also need the plan.

Success comes from many places, but entrepreneurs usually take primary responsibility for themselves. After all, there wouldn't be much anything call 'lucky' if they hadn't started it.

Personally, I think luck is a mixture of hard work, good timing, motivation and determination.

Be ready to take advantage of luck

CHAPTER FOURTEEN

JUDITH'S JEWELERY STORY

After 46 years of happy marriage, Judith was widowed at the age of 71. She continued to cry after her husband died and locked herself in. She refused to leave her house, except to go and buy the necessary supplies. She put her closest friend aside. She only spoke with her only daughter, her son-in-law, and her three grandchildren living abroad.

A year passed, and she was invited to visit the family by her daughter, and it took a persuasive campaign to bring her to New York for the visit.

Judith's visited the fashion boutiques during her visit to New York. Judith had a lot of passion and appreciation for fashion. Her friends are always quick to praise her beautiful, fashionable lifestyle and that she has been fortunate enough to have good tastes of fashionable clothes and jewellery.

Judith's once went to a jewellery store just to look and admire the range of jewellery, and remember the good time she was shopping in the most exclusive boutiques and buying designer clothes and accessories.

The shop owner approached her as she was about to leave and complimented her on the jewellery she was wearing while asking where she bought the jewellery. Judith, not shocked by the question, replied that some European jewellers had designed and created this jewellery especially for her.

The discussion continued at a nearby cafe, where the owner of the jewellery store asked her if she would be willing to send the catalogues of the jewellers she knows.

Judith's approached some designers she knew on her return home and asked for catalogues of their current collection, which she sent to Samantha (the store owner from New York). Judith received an order for jewellery valued at $ 30,000 after less than a week. She immediately recognized the opportunity to start a business, and with the encouragement of Samantha, who has become her close friend, Judith started selling jewelleries to another outlet that Samantha introduces her to.

Judith's currently employs two employees and six agents in the United States, with annual sales of over $2 million. After three years at age 74, she is enjoying a successful business and now travels more often to visit his family.

Judith's story is unique in her opportunity, but the ability to identify an opportunity is up to us and all the time that we see an opportunity coming our way we just need to write them down.

JUDITH'S'S TIP

- You must be able to know the difference between a dream and fantasy, cross the divide between vision and your decisions, balance hope with facts, and know where you are and where you are going to be a successful entrepreneur.
- The way you respond to challenges makes the difference between success and failure.
- You are responsible as an entrepreneur and any decisions you make will affect the business, your life and your family. The good news is that you have complete autonomy and freedom of choice over your choices, but know that you will

> have to live with their repercussions if your decision is not correct.

Your Goals as An Entrepreneur

The purpose of this chapter is to discuss the importance of having business goals and the processes involved in achieving those goals.

The goals are all-powerful and influential; they can focus all your energy on getting the desired result.

A desired result in business will be profitability.

What is the real meaning of business goals?

Well, there are quite a few explanations, but to sum it up, setting goals always gives you the power to stay focused on intention and allows you to prepare yourself, and you can do something about that when you have it.

Goal setting is an essential part of finding the right business for you. After all, if your business isn't meeting your personal goals, you probably won't be happy every morning waking up and trying to make your business a success. This may stop you from putting the necessary effort into making your idea work.

OBJECTIVE → PLAN → ACTION

What helps make your dreams come true is implementing a strategy. Those who can recognize their own strengths and abilities and then set goals that will expand their abilities without ever exceeding them are the world's most effective individuals and the best managers.

There is a fine line between goals that are too simple to achieve and goals that are probably beyond your control. The goal setting method allows you in your business as in your life to choose your path.

You will know where to focus your energies, knowing exactly what you want to accomplish. You will also easily notice distractions in your path that would otherwise attract you.

It is when people realize their fundamental interests, aspirations and ambitions that they gain a sense of hope and freedom.

In a seminar I gave to small business owners who were in trouble, I asked them a simple question:

"What are your business and personal goals?"

To my great surprise, only three knew how to define their business and personal goals. The rest could not define their vision, their goals or even their expectations.

This is probably one of the main reasons that their businesses have been struggling.

Nevertheless, I feel that goals are not worth the paper they are written on if one's values are not determined first.

The definition of establishing and hitting a target in its simplest form is:

You need to determine what your goal really is.

And you have to describe it in detail.

Then you need to specify the steps by which you plan to reach the goal, and finally, in order to reach your goal, you need to set a deadline or a time limit.

Values, passion and desire are an essential component of success

Much of the reading I've done shows that goals go hand in hand with achievement. I would add that values, enthusiasm and desire are the necessary ingredients for success.

It is therefore important that your goals, aspirations and beliefs are a set of principles that must exist and maintain harmony with the concept of your goals. Your performance will become a part of you with them, and you are a part of it.

Define The Company Objective

The method of setting goals can be likened to a long-distance drive.

Without knowing where you were going and why you wanted to go, you wouldn't dream of planning the trip.

You would have determined the path and you would have an idea of how long it would take to reach your destination.

Sounds familiar, eh?

Ok, goal setting uses the same ideas except that you are the vehicle in this situation and your business is the journey

How to organize goals

Be Specific

Goals should be specific, to determine exactly what you want.

It is not enough to pretend that you want to make more money. How much more money do you want to earn?

You should also write down the priorities. About 3% of adults write down their goals, and these people have achieved several times more than the rest.

Entrepreneurs who wrote down their goals are 11 times more likely than those who didn't write down their goals and have them in mind to achieve what they set out to do.

Measurable steps

Goals must be measurable. If the goal is not measurable, how do you know you can accomplish it?

For example, when you say how much money you want to earn, you have something to calculate how and when you get it, you will know it.

Create a list

To achieve the goal, make a list of everything you can think of and do. Just write down each point, big and small.

This shift makes sure mental gears are in such a way that now you come to believe more that it is possible.

Act

You need to be impatient, capable, and ready to take action to achieve your goal. Your goal will not be achieved without clear and continuous action

Put your idea in motion and do something right away.

Now do something

Do something that will not be delayed, what I found is if you hesitate to take action on your plan, chances are you will never take action at all, it will just become a dry piece of paper. Taking action that will essentially bring your goals to life.

Accessible

Goals can stretch you out, but they're still achievable. It will not be motivating if the target is out of control.

A 69-year-old man, for example, who has no political experience and wants to set a goal of becoming president of the United States within the next five years, sets a goal that is not achievable.

However, it is possible to set a goal for other civic activities, such as showing up at a local office or working on a political campaign.

Be limited in time

It must be time-bound to make a goal compelling. When setting your goals, the question to ask yourself is: "When?"

It's always possible to change the date, but it gives you something to work on and it's motivating.

For your brain, a deadline is essential. Your brain requires a deadline.

Have the desire

There must be a strong desire for the goal to be achieved. You will not achieve your goals without desire.

Clear minded

And you should always be open-minded as you follow your goal because you may need to change your path in the middle.

Things may arise, obstacles may arise, new knowledge may arise, and you may want to tweak or change your course.

Goal achievement process

1. Set a goal.

2. List the resources needed to achieve this.

3. List the assets you currently have to make this possible

4. Identify the blocks or barriers that stand in the way.

5. List all the important milestones to be crossed along the way (with dates).

6. List the actions required by the specified date to reach the first milestone.

7. Build when you reach your goal as a reward or celebration.

> *Friedrich Nietzsche, German philosopher, wrote:*
> "He who has a way of life can bear almost any how."

CHAPTER FIFTEEN

NADINE BOOKKEEPING SERVICES STORY

Hello, my name is Nadine, I felt like I had to do something a few months after I retired. I was okay with the idea of retirement, but I can't stand the idea of not working at all. I certainly wanted my income to continue to increase. What does a woman like me do after 40 years of public service?

I decided to study bookkeeping and develop my own small bookkeeping service business. My needs would be met by this form of activity while leaving plenty of free time for family, friends, hobbies, travel, or whatever I like.

A bookkeeper can perform a wide range of administrative and clerical activities, but "keeping the books", especially the journals and records that document all financial transactions, is the primary goal associated with accounting. A bookkeeper is a person whose job is to monitor the financial affairs of a company. Bookkeeping is required by any organization and self- employed individual.

My idea was to target baby boomer entrepreneurs with my service because I understand their needs and the issues they face. Most importantly, they need personalized service, a friendly face, a lot of patience and flexible service charges.

Working from home, I started my own small business with nothing more than a computer, fax machine, and the proper accounting software.

I run my own profitable business today, with many satisfied clients, most of whom are mature entrepreneurs. I reduce my costs so that I can market my services at a low and flexible price.

There is a growing commercial market looking for what I offer.

I love what I do and I know I support people, that's what makes me tick.

NADINE TIP

- Confidence and enthusiasm are not enough to run a business. Therefore, before starting your business, it is very important that you spend time collecting data with courses and workshops, or with literature and articles.
- Old age is an advantage in accounting because it requires the confidence of the business owner to file the accountant's secrets regarding all his affairs and money in some cases, the wisdom and experience of old age are a suitable ground for building trust between the business owner and the accountant.

Reflection and Application: Determine Your Goal

Many of you have goals in mind, but you also need more clarity, guidelines, and a plan of action. However, some of you don't even know where to start and the very setting of goals blocks them. The purpose of this task is to help you identify your goals so that you can work on a clear plan of action, stay focused, and get the most out of your business.

It is when people realize their fundamental interests, aspirations and ambitions that they gain a sense of hope and freedom.

QUESTIONS FOR DETERMINE YOUR GOAL

- What do you really want?

- When you have it, how would you feel?
- If you were to live this goal now, how will your life be different?
- If you don't, what's the danger?
- What will it take for you to get there?
- What are you going to get out of it?
- What are your choices?
- Right now, what goal would make the biggest difference in your life?
- What else do you want in your life? (Make a list)
- What do you want less in your life to have?
- What will be the main outcome of achieving the goals?
- Do you have the power to achieve this goal?
- Are you inspired and energized by your goals?
- Can you imagine yourself having achieved your goal?
- Do you have any doubts?
- Are your standards realistic?
- What comes naturally to you?
- What achieved goal of yours would you like to be part of your legacy?

Take a notebook, scribble down your ideas and add your own useful questions

CHAPTER SIXTEEN

ALEX'S 'S PRIVATE TEACHING STORY

Alex, with a long and successful high-tech career behind him. Six months after his retirement, he began to realize what boredom really meant.

"I missed the crowds and the activity, and when there are no issues to solve, you get bored too," he said.

I'm sixty-eight, financially, "OK" wanted to use my math skills to support and educate students by providing private tutoring services while looking to do something exciting with my life, something that would excite me.

As an entrepreneur, I quickly realized that it was a whole industry, with a massive market and a strong demand for their children from parents, I recognized the opportunity to combine operation, participation and profit, so everyone will benefit, everyone will be happy.

It takes some preparation to start a private tutoring business and usually starts on a budget and gradually expands the business over time. Tutors are always in demand to help struggling students keep up with their lessons or to stimulate the minds of talented learners. Sometimes students need tutors to help them pass important exams or prepare for graduate school.

So, I had to turn to two of my colleagues, Tommy, retired, professor of science and physics, and Peter, a friend of mine and associate of a high-tech company. We started a business that offered tutoring services to students.

Private teachers are always in demand, Alex says, "for students who have study difficulties or those who want to improve their grades." "Parents, as you know, don't save on helping their children."

The current situation is different from what it once was. The motivating principles for engaging a private tutor are ambition and realizing the potential of the learner. In fact, the high demand has created a market for parents concerned with the success of their children and their future. This generation is more aware and achievable, and therefore this business model has become well recognized.

"This same business starts with a very low budget and grows gradually as needed. There are enough qualified teachers who are happy to work for you and supplement their income," Alex's continues with his convincing arguments.

"In small groups, we have developed learning models, increased the possibilities of assistance, and thus reduced the cost of private tutoring without losing the concept and quality of the private lesson."

"Believe me, everyone knows it, and everyone wins. The unique and creative teaching methods we have developed help students interact with learning topics in a personal and focused way, thanks to our professional background and experience."

"Our students learn to build instruments to understand and internalize subjects by the end of the day. They don't just learn to take tests."

"In recent times, markets have grown globally through online courses, and there are companies offering private, publicly traded courses, who have created innovative teaching methods and sold franchises.". All private lessons are on the increase in the western world "

ALEX'S TIP

- To stay up to date with the material that is being learned, it is important to keep in touch with teachers in schools, so that teachers can get to know you and also send you students who need tutoring.
- It is essential that you impart your knowledge to students if you have the knowledge and the opportunity to teach. You will certainly get a lot of satisfaction.
- You already have within you the potential you need to be successful. A plan is what you need.

VALUES

The emphasis is on setting goals and achieving them, but the issue of values has not been properly addressed.

In business, values are your fundament beliefs.

These guiding principles guide actions and will help you understand the distinction between right and wrong.

Our values shape our relationships, our behaviour, our decisions and who we are.

Values are so essential because our relationships, attitudes, decisions and who we are, are deeply shaped by them.

So as an entrepreneur, it is literally difficult to create the business you want without knowing your values because there is no basis on which to develop it.

Young entrepreneurs often do not understand why, being focused, they do not achieve these goals.

This is because, based on outward appearances, they want to make their priorities what others want from them or what they think they want or should want for themselves.

Values are fundamentally reflected in the behaviour and relationship with your immediate environment, family, friends, and customers.

Your choices and values reflect you.

Therefore, by describing your goals, expressing them will ensure and advance their achievement.

The chances of success without them are uncertain.

It is therefore essential that you first assess your values and seek to incorporate them into your goals.

Ask yourself the following controversial questions to define your values:

QUESTIONS OF VALUES

1. What are the core values in your life that make you feel more complete?
2. Depending on your lifestyle, which values should you be part of?
3. What are the ideals that it is essential that you incorporate into your business so that you feel that your priorities are fully realized?
4. What values do others praise you for?
5. What are the missing values that make you feel incomplete?
6. What does your heart say?

CHAPTER SEVENTEEN

FLORA SOAP MAKING STORY

Hi, my name is Flora. I have been making scented soaps at home for over five years. I became a widower at the age of sixty-five, after forty-eight years of marriage.

Soap making has grown from a hobby to a very competitive profession that often attracts new talent. To learn the professional way on soap making, the trick is to how to find the best soap making recipes, ingredient list, a good instructions manual and expert advice.

I've always dreamed of starting my own soap making business, but I didn't know where to start. While it can be very difficult to start a business, it takes time and thoughtful planning to establish a successful business.

I signed up for the home-made soap class at my friend's suggestion. The good thing about this business is that it does not require a large investment. Oils with charming and varied aromas are the raw materials. Soap can be produced at home in the kitchen. The mechanism itself is fun and mixes science and art.

Knowledge and openness to other toiletries is very strong, and therefore the demand for such a product is excellent.

After five years, I rented a warehouse in the suburbs of my hometown. The warehouse serves as a processing plant and a workshop and classroom location. In terms of production and marketing, I employ five retired women to help out. We operate in a sector where the industrial rivalry is high but we have a high turnover. After I started the company, I saw that it was a successful business that existed in its own right and with confidence and devotion.

FLORA TIP

- Many people assume that the difference between a successful business and an unsuccessful business is only money (capital). While money is an important factor, the attitude and confidence of the entrepreneur in himself is just as important to the success of the business.

Reflection and Application: Determine Your Values

Determining your values will help you describe and affirm what is really important to you in life. The question of values is often overlooked because it seems to be a huge and difficult question to resolve. The term "values" is used too quickly and too loosely. Values and goals are also mixed. Where are we going to start? Start early by asking thought-provoking questions.

Mark ten values out of the list that you use in your life.

- Responsibility
- Freedom
- Competitiveness
- Recognition
- Wisdom
- Self-Respect
- Friendship

- Culture
- Creativity
- Affection
- Adventure
- Involvement
- Achievement
- Wealth
- Cooperation
- Economic Security
- Fame
- Power
- Integrity
- Personal Development
- Family Happiness
- Pleasure

List out other values that you found useful that is not on the list.

Select your top 3 values and define what these values mean to you

1.

2.

3.

Take a notebook, scribble down your ideas and add your own useful questions

CHAPTER EIGHTEEN

BERT'S STORY AS A FAMILY HISTORIAN

Accelerated technology has created various possibilities for communication between individuals, but this advanced accessibility reduces intergenerational contact. On social media, young people spend more time surfing and chatting than with their families, the talk is virtual, the tradition of family history disappears and adults do not tell family stories anymore. Family history is becoming lost and gone without "telling your son".

Bert retired at the age of sixty-seven, having been a teacher all his adult life. "I quickly realized that the idea of retirement and living on a retiring allowance was not right for me," said Bert. Without a specific direction for me to continue my life, I began to find my way.

One day after he had a heart attack, when I visited my father in the hospital, I realized that I knew little about my parents' childhood. They didn't tell me, and I didn't ask, and I realized the great lack of knowledge, even though I was from another generation.

They must have had an interesting story about themselves, because they emigrate from Russia. What about the extended family and their friends who were left behind in Russia?

That same week, before their health deteriorated and their memory failed them, I decided to document my parents' story, their life story and that of their families and friends.

The work of documenting and writing my family history was a turning point in my life, I fell in love with the process and the outcome, and I realized that my own case could become a sustainable business.

I approached three of my friends who love written words. They were enthusiastic, and so we set off without any prior experience in starting a business. There was only one thing we had in common, and we just had to believe that something good would come out of it.

We hired a mentor who helped us and taught us how to turn our idea into a business.

Our job, explains Bert, is to create a narrative out of someone's history and rephrase it as stories.

And why do you only employ retirees? I asked. "In writing the family history, our advantage is our age. The majority of our clients are our age. We come from a familiar background and are sensitive and intuitive enough to know how deep we can dig into the narrator's life and when to stop digging. During interviews, as most of us have the same mindset, we are in contact with the client and offer him a space of comfort and safety."

As Bert goes on to explain, "the important thing that the family historian offers his clients is to institutionalize their story and pass it on to their loved ones. It is a very moving message of reflection and reconciliation, of happy moments and the continuation of a chain through our writing tools that the whole family shares and appreciates.

- Family history provides links.
- it reminds us where we come from.
- it's good for your children.
- it informs your health choices.
- it encourages compassion.

In the reality of every nation and every country, the role of the family historian is important, commemorating the history of gone generations and thus linking an intergenerational bond between grandparents and grandchildren.

Through the company that I founded; I have a mission. "

> ## BERT'S TIP
>
> - You actually hold a mirror in front of you when you have your own business; everything that happens in the company reflects you.
> - We can live our lives authentically and satisfactorily if we listen to our feelings and make a real assessment of our strengths and weaknesses, and make the right choices.
> - You must clarify the issues related to your opportunities at this stage in your life, the goals you are trying to achieve, the resources you need to achieve these goals, respect the values that serve you and get rid of those that do not serve, without guilt.

TAKE ACTION

"Vision without action ... is just a dream. Action without a vision is just the passing of time Vision with action can change the world" (Joel A. Baker)

Nothing without action happens.

Creating action begins with tapping into the reason behind what you want and deciding what action is necessary to obtain your desire goal.

Sometimes people think goal setting is the end of the process. On the contrary, this is only the beginning. Once the strategy is formulated, you will need to create an action plan to achieve the desired goal.

You now know what you want to accomplish; you have defined your goals and values; it is time to create an action plan. This plan will create a structure for you to work with. You will have a roadmap to follow by creating an action plan, as well as a process for tracking achievements and challenges.

To achieve a goal, your desire is not enough. To achieve a goal, you must have the courage, the will and a plan of action.

Break Your Goal Into Series Sub-Goals

Remember, if it's broken down into a series of sub-goals, it's much easier to achieve a goal. Each sub-goal should lead you to the ultimate goal with its particular deadline.

Also, you need to tackle this issue sequentially, completing one sub-goal before moving on to the next.

A targeted goal without action is just a hypothesis and nothing more.

To support your action, get resources

You have to put in place a structure to support your actions; it is an important step in the process of achieving your goals.

You will benefit by preparing in advance before embarking on our journey to be successful in the process.

Create a list of what you will need to do, what information you need, who can help you, and other resources you need to support your action.

Build a support team. Surround yourself with people who will be supportive and helpful.

CHAPTER NINETEEN

NANCY'S CONSULTING STORY

For businesses, organizations, and individuals looking for advice, ideas and solutions to technical problems or dilemmas, knowledge and experience are valuable resources. When used in a professional environment to offer consulting services in your area of specialization, you bring with you many years of work in the area in which you have worked and specialized. A good consultant requires skills and experience; these are attributes that you have.

We can find a hive of specialties in the consulting sector. It is inhabited by hundreds of fields, ranging from marketing, financial, technical, agriculture or textile industry. They offer advice to an endless list of services. Your advantage, in addition to the theoretical expertise in the field on which you are advising, is that in the light of your years of experience you can really integrate suggestions and conclusions of reports by combining theory and action.

It has been discovered in interviews with baby boomers that many of them do not understand and are not even aware of the information they have acquired throughout their lives in their field of activity.

Hello, my name is Nancy and I have been running a toddler day-care for over thirty years. I continued to research new approaches during my years of work and update myself with information applicable to this area of work.

The telephones did not stop ringing after I retired. Many parents continued to call and ask for advice on matters relating to the care, schooling and education of their children. I decided to create a consulting firm a year after my retirement. I started a counselling company for parents of preschool children with the help of a business mentor. I widened the circle of my clients to include parents and grandparents, becoming a grandmother myself and understanding the needs of grandparents.

Today I have come a long way and hired four other counsellors that I had personally trained. I have given parent and grandparent classes and seminars for these counsellors, and am in the process of writing a parenting guide for young children. The art of therapy is a source of great pleasure and interest, according to Nancy.

It was a huge step forward towards what was a fulfilling profession for me. When setting up the clinic, the expertise and specialized skills that I had developed over the years of training were made available to parents and grandparents. I brought the value of my continued development and on-the-job learning while continuing to practice. Not only my presence and my attention, my care and encouragement, my interest and my dedication, but an opportunity to grow together in a relationship like no other I have offered to my clients. It seemed like a great gift for my clients. Some consumers would never have had the privilege of being listened to before, and many will never have gained quality time and dedicated attention uniquely to them and their concerns. It was gratifying to be supportive and make it go away.

NANCY'S TIP

- Don't underestimate the talent you have. We have a human propensity to not understand the true value of our abilities and experience, but to note that what you think is normal does not necessarily happen in others.

Reflection And Application: Taking Action

The following questions will support you in taking the appropriate action at the right time.

- What is the first step for you?
- What should happen now?
- How could you have made your goal measurable?
- What is your time frame?
- What is your priority?
- Who can help you and in what area?
- What obstacles will probably hold you back?
- What three acts you would do this week that would make sense?
- What would you do to inspire yourself to achieve your goals?
- Are you committed or are you just trying this?

Take a notebook, scribble down your ideas and add your own useful questions

1. What mechanisms do you need to put in place to achieve your goal?
2. Do you have the required strengths and capabilities?

CHAPTER TWENTY

DONNA'S STORY OF PATCHWORK QUILTS COUTURE

Hello, I'm Donna, a hospital nurse and a retiree. As a hobby, I started my quilt sewing business at the age of sixty-four. I teach and lecture at seminars and community centres. Today at the age of 75 and sell my products online from my website all over the world. I was nervous and bored when I retired. My friend gave me a present, a guide to making quilts on my sixty-fourth birthday.

Patchwork quilts are beautiful to look at, own and make. In decades past, one of the first art projects that many people learned to create was to make a quilt from fabric. Getting started is very easy and every time I complete a quilting project, my creative abilities develop.

I quickly discovered that making quilts does not require prior knowledge; there are short, inexpensive courses for sewing training and blanket making. I learned from my testing that the production investment is minimal, all that is needed is a cutting board and roller knife, scissors, ruler and a sewing machine. It is not expensive to use sewing machines; you can use a second-hand sewing machine, as long as it is in good condition.

My 78-year-old husband, Greg, helped me with product marketing. I wanted to specialize in baby quilt patchwork. There are many types of blankets that can be created from simple patches, colour variations, different patterns to different fabric styles and fabric shapes. The remaining raw materials are purchased from fabric stores and clothing producers and often we equally receive the remaining waste from clothing manufacturers for free. Often times we cut off old patches from clothes, we have a business we haven't spent much on, we make a living from it and we enjoy every moment.

DONNA'S TIP

- Your life will be transformed by the spirit of enterprise; it will affect your self-esteem, your family, your wealth, your well-being, your future, your aspirations and your dreams. Above all, entrepreneurship requires courage and imagination.

PRACTICAL TOOLS

Why are you interested in starting a small business?

What motivates you?

You need to write down and analyse the reasons for your desire to run your own business before you even let your thoughts come out of the front door. In addition, you can examine your own personal characteristics, circumstances, skills and experience.

Then look for a niche for your business and analyse your market.

Your niche is defined as place, status or activity where you are most comfortable or best suited.

In other words, you are looking for a business that makes you feel good that you would be able to create and grow, and you are also looking for a specific need that you can fill in the population.

Write down the answers to the following questions to decide if your basic concept is workable:

- Provide a concise overview of the business you want to create.
- Name the product or service you are offering.
- Describe the unfulfilled need in the marketplace that you are addressing.
- Describe the current market for your product or service, particularly to determine whether or not demand exceeds supply.
- Determine if, based on its particular characteristics, the product or service can be competitive in today's market.

MARKET ANALYSIS

Once you believe that you have found a niche in the business world for yourself, that is, you think your product and service can be competitive; you need to take a closer look at the market you are going to serve.

1. Who will your customers be and what will they need from you?

2. Do you know the exact geographic region you will be serving?

3. Are there any particular religious traditions or values that you should be aware of?

4. Will you be providing goods and services at rates that your customers are willing to pay and would your products and services be comparable to what is currently offered in the market in terms of price and quality?

5. Have you developed a promotional program that effectively targets your specific market?

CUSTOMER RELATIONSHIP SKILLS

For the success of any small business, customer support is of the utmost importance. Studies in today's business world have shown that attracting a new customer will cost six times more than keeping an existing one.

It seems that customer service has become very impersonal with the outsourcing of customer service departments, telephones answered by machines, and email. This is where you can have an advantage over large organizations.

So how do you show your customers how valuable they are to you and ensure their return? Treat customers the way they want to be treated. Identify the companies in which you enjoyed doing business and list the specifics of the experience.

Another successful strategy is to behave like you're the only one the customer will interact with their business (and you just might be in the case of a small home business) and the reputation of the business rests only on your shoulders. Imagine that every customer is also the most important customer. If the customer reacts well to you and feels valued, then you have probably earned their loyalty.

CHAPTER TWENTY-ONE

ALFRED'S STORY: A RESEARCH USING THE INTERNET

By its very nature, the enormous amount of knowledge that exists on the Internet, including social media, is an invitation to a growing appetite for research services. Businesses, organizations, and agencies seek diverse and in-depth knowledge, and it's a simple job to consider the availability of current information for the benefit of all. However, in the absence of trained staff, time, money or technical expertise, knowledge seekers prefer to go to outside to seek out companies specializing in internet analysis on a range of topics, such as studies, market research, product research, related product information, competitor information and marketing practices, means of sale, market demographics, etc.

These lone-wolf businesses have been simplified thanks to the Internet, which allows virtual sales and purchases as well as jobs. It also makes starting and running a business less physically demanding. It has helped people with constraints and waning energy start successful businesses.

The localization task is a didactic task that involves the ability to scan and summarize, to differentiate the tasteless from the good, and to refine the importance of the necessary information. Alfred, a retiree from the Department of Defense, told me that the life of a retiree is monotonous; "I felt the urge to find other ways to re-spark my life. "

One day I browsed through the site that fascinated me, a company in the United States that offers Internet research services.

Great idea, I was thinking of myself and a curious man like me, I checked and unearthed other companies that offer this type of internet service as of this day and for a month.

I learned about the range of services they provide, their marketing techniques and their business model. I have also learned that knowledge is an expensive commodity and there is an enormous amount of information available on websites, blogs and social business networks, so there must be a demand from consumers using the services analysis as a product.

I called some of my friends who worked in various companies and noticed that these services were in high demand. From there the road was short as I wanted to start a business to provide information on the internet, I hired the services of Mentor to support me in retrospect in the early stages of running the business, the overview most significant about how to start the business was that inf.

At the age of 69, Alfred started his business. Today, the company employs around 40 part-time students. "These are the long arms of the tasks of localizing, reading, rewriting, editing until the finished material is submitted to the appropriate needs of the end customer," the secret of my success "is the result of professionalizing a certain domain on the Internet. "It saves me valuable research time, shortens customer service delivery time, saves expense, and generates reputation."

ALFRED'S TIP

- You have to find as much knowledge as possible before starting a business, now in the Internet age; the work is easy, but requires perseverance and discipline. Do market research, talk to people, and learn more about entrepreneurship, financing, pricing, and marketing. Ask questions and don't be discouraged to seek help if you don't know anything, and the more you know, the more you know, the more you know.

Business Concept (Preparation And Formulation)

You have entered the moment of truth at this point. You have chosen to join the entrepreneurial community and start your own business. You are probably wondering,

What now and how do I go about it? "

HOW DO I START? "

The reality about this is that any new business begins with an idea, or a series of ideas that is generated in our mind.

Fortunately, without investing a lot, it now becomes very easy to start a business from scratch.

This chapter explains how to get started and how to simply create a unique business concept.

GENERATE A BUSINESS CONCEPT

From the need to accomplish a predetermined goal, an idea can be generated or formed. Following an event or a small talk that ignites your line of thinking.

An opportunity that come your way, or something else that you hadn't thought of before.

It could be something you've always done for fun and didn't know it could be your source of income.

Anything new or unique means an innovative idea; you're talking about the first of such idea.

Original ideas, while necessarily creative, may already exist, but from a different point of view to the way it is conceived by you. You have added or modified another layer of strategy that it becomes an original concept with its characteristics.

The original concepts just require a little imagination on your part.

In reality, the innovation involved consists in developing new links between established concepts.

This is very exciting, because it implies that the imagination instantly seems less scary: we can all connect things that already exist, right?

IMPLEMENT YOUR IDEA

Each of us has one good idea or another at specific times in our life, and there are often multiples of these ideas.

Only a few percent of people with great ideas put their ideas in motion.

We report our ideas to friends, relatives, or co-workers at some point in everyone's life, and the response we get is it's a great idea, you should do something about it.

"I don't have time," "I don't have the resources," "I don't have enough money," "Difficult to implement," "I'm too old." This are some of many often-strange reasons that emerges, as we get older, and as the number of ideas increases, so does the number of excuses.

What are you waiting for today? Start working on those ideas now.

TRANSFORM ALL "NO" ANSWERS TO BIG "YES"

This is the moment when you take a moment to continue our virtual conversation and turn all the 'no' that has been part of you so far into a major 'yes'.

It would shock you to see that a constructive terminological change produces a positive understanding that is more open to action, change and initiative.

More than once you get to know a good and surprising idea of its simplicity, grab your head and say to yourself, "How did I not think about it before now?"

You hear more than once from someone who thought of an idea similar to yours but they executed it, but unlike you that did nothing, they came up with success. This is a justification for you to try to execute the concept that you have in you.

What are the things that make you wake up smiling every morning?

There is this opinion that has been circulating for many years that entrepreneurs should be engaged in what they know and not what they want.

Recognize today that this opinion is deeply flawed. Entrepreneurs have to handle the things they want, love and burn the desire to engage in them.

So always ask yourself, when you are formulating that business idea, what you want to do, what task will make you happy.

What is that very one thing that will please you and make you lose your sense of time without getting lost?

Which operation will allow the tasks to be carried out effortlessly? What will make you wake up with a smile on your face every morning?

If you haven't thought about asking yourself these questions in the past, do some research on your own, find answers, and assess your arrangements at the same time.

Your business idea involves a journey of self-discovery to plan and formulate it.

Recognizing and understanding your heart's desire and tilt will catch up with your beliefs and values, with your way of thinking.

The point at which the definition does not deviate from your thoughts and feelings informs you that this is "the one", then you need to check profitability, expenses, marketability, growth potential and management capacity. There is no going back or second guessing at this point.

LISTEN

Ideas must be evaluated, and strategy formulated for an effective implementation. There are listening levels which are mainly:

- To listen to the market.
- To listen to potential customers.
- The more you listen, the more you understand and be able to respond and behave in a consistent way in order to drive your thoughts.

Business philosophy calls for assessment and criticism from multiple perspectives. There will also be major inconsistencies and variations in your interpretation of the concept and how it will be perceived by your targeted customers. Be prepared to pay for it.

A business viability analysis that measures the product in terms of realism and attractiveness is the main step in assessing your company's prospects for survival in market volatility, whether your business is selling a physical product or it's a service provider. It's time to act after you've formulated and prepared.

Your Passion And Your Desire

So, choosing something that you are passionate about is the first step, and indeed the most important step. You have to be really enthusiastic about your own ideas and take a keen interest in them.

Answer the following questions to describe your passion and desire:

1. Do you understand your passion and your desire to do something?
2. And if so, what is that passion?
3. Try to describe it in depth.
4. How to harness your passion and where?
5. Who and what could help you apply your passion?

It can be colleagues, peers, family members, practitioners. They will help you make important decisions and make the right choices.

MOTIVATION AND INTEREST

At this point in your life, what are the things that attracts or motivates you?

Along with dedication and consideration, the business concept should convey fun behaviour.

An idea that does not have the required spark will not generate the momentum needed to start the work process, especially at your age. This is a true assertion.

YOU

At different stages in your personal and professional life, your business is a representation of yourself, your values, and the amount of expertise, abilities, experience and relationships you have gained. All of these are accelerators of your success in your business.

YOUR TARGET

Several preliminary questions as part of a required feasibility study

1. Pinpoint and spell out your goal.

2. Do you have faith in this?
3. Is it achievable?

Your initial roadmap is these leading questions. Therefore, at this point, your responses these posers are primarily intuition and instinct. Your experience and expertise are your hidden arsenal of weapons. Trust them and use them in the process of defining the target, its meaning, and the decision to enforce it in that order.

PRODUCT

Your product must offer a solution and a response to those who request it. Customers look for solutions to specific problems or needs - providing them with a particular product or service that will meet their problem or need. Your advantage over your competition will be that your product will be unique and will exactly meet your customer's needs.

The "WOW" effect

What makes your product special and convincing for your clients to choose it?

Consider the reasons that will excite your customers, the "Wow" effect. You have to ask yourself where to focus your commercial advantages for your business, where will you stand out from your competition.

The following questions will explain this as you answer the questions, trying to position yourself in the shoes of the customers.

1. What can I say that will meet the needs of customers?
2. What I can offer that has not necessarily been offered, or that has not yet been suggested?
3. What a current customer has not yet been offered?
4. What is more important to the customer than the price of the goods?

5. What is the experience that is important to me as a consumer in the process of finding and buying a product?
6. Are service and shopping experience enough?

Each response should include an additional and special component of added value that does not exist or has not yet been considered or addressed. This added value has a vital weight in the ability to redirect focus from another business idea (which was floating around in the sea of ideas) to a valuable innovative path that needs to be sold.

Any organization that wants to succeed should embrace this business concept, and the purpose or motive for developing it at an advanced age is not important.

In short, use your instincts, principles, and intuition to decide what type of business is best for you, whether it's physical goods or services. Your business plan will begin to take shape this way. And you will find that you are managing a method of selling a business idea to yourself, just like any sales process that starts with defining the need.

CHAPTER TWENTY-TWO

THE STORY OF CYRIL'S YOUTH CARE

Cyril is a sixty-eight-year-old retiree. He was a software developer before his retirement. "It all started with a briefing report of my grandson," Cyril said with an indulgent smile on his face.

My grandson bragged that his grandfather was an internet expert to his classmates, and when the rumour circulated in the teacher's room, someone thought it was right to invite me talk to students about the dangers of the Internet, cyberbullying and how to prevent them.

This led to my giving lectures at my grandchildren's school. But the rumour spread to other schools and I was asked to give lectures too. After a few months had passed, the news of my teaching reached several social organizations among them, organizations that are concerned with young people at risk of degenerating into delinquency.

There are young people between the ages of 14 and 18 who have been kicked out of education systems for different reasons and who even have "intimate relationships with repressive systems".

I have heard intimate and heart-breaking stories from these young people. The sacred work of their guardians and the powerlessness of government agencies that I have come to know and cherish. I visited youth centres, and I learned and internalized what seemed to be a great social wound for our culture in particular.

Just like that, this moment of continuous insight was kind of wake-up call for me on a long journey of discovery. I decided to create an organization that would try to bring some of the young people back into society to incorporate them. It's not too late for that.

I have to confess that I was shocked by the spirit of volunteering to which I was introduced in my appeal for support and contributions from friends and from other citizens, and it was very convenient for me to excite and volunteer some of my fellow pensioners who were happy to lend a hand and devote their time and expertise to a society whose fate was not better.

Our non-profit organization has gained a deep working experience, and we have expanded and opened branches around the nation through its programs that have rescued many of these young people from helplessness.

The priorities of our organization are as follows:

1. Build an alternative to the life of street gangs.
2. Preventive measures aimed at stopping you from crime.
3. Locate and minimize child abuse by adults.
4. Give at-risk youth the capacity and resources to integrate and have a positive impact on society.
5. Academic assistance and improvement of personal skills by volunteer teachers.
6. Support for the transition to vocational training systems.
7. Promotion and improvement of personal and interpersonal communication skills.
8. Identify leadership and improve on it.
9. Restore confidence and its diverse representation in society in the establishment.

The whole association is focused on volunteering, using mainly retirees from various professional backgrounds, everyone will be in our association, each voice has an echo, you will find business leaders, retirees of public companies, engineers, lawyers, accountants, and several volunteers from all professions, community and private businesses that have become part of the association.

"What inspired me to start a non-profit organization in my old age, like many important decisions in my life," said Cyril, "was a mixture of desire to change fate and the frustration with the current situation of society. But as soon as I decided to set up the organization that takes care of young people at risk to degenerate into delinquency. As an entrepreneur, I realized that the potential for the success of the project depends on the use of correct strategy and action."

With the enthusiasm of a little boy who has been released into a toy store, Cyril talks about the organization and its events with sparkling eyes, and sometimes during our long conversations I have noticed the dampness in his eyes, evidence of secret excitement.

It was clear that he loved every moment with a confidence in the road's fairness. He clearly answered me when I raised his perception of the ideals that inspired him: "You are absolutely right, it is pure pleasure, and I am full of expectations every morning to go out with the association. And I feel like I've reinvented myself, I've never felt more complete with myself than in this chapter of my life.

"CYRIL'S TIP

- For the creation of a more just and equitable society, the contribution of the retiree is important. The social entrepreneur contributes directly or indirectly to the economy and to culture.
- Entrepreneurship at an older age also coincides with another theme - the urge to give back to society - that arises later in life. Research reveals that half of those who want to be middle-aged entrepreneurs still want to solve social needs and solve social problems at the same time.

CHAPTER TWENTY-THREE

WRAP UP

This book is a guide that describes the action and development of those who decide to start their life as an entrepreneur after retirement.

This book has tried to combine personal stories with technical instructions and lines of action.

Guidelines for Small Business Success

1) Make a plan.

You need to find ways to distinguish your business from that of your competition.

To choose you over the more developed places of business, your customers need strong, solid reasons.

In your area, consider the market, what customers need and want, and what the competition is currently offering.

Take a clear look at the strengths and weaknesses of your business.

To build a plan of attack, take advantage of this experience.

Don't let yourself slip into the old pit of trying to be everyone's thing. Locate your niche.

2) Before you even open your doors, create a business plan and budget and update it at least once a year.

If you have a vision for the future, you will be able to reach higher expectations rather than just going from day to day, hoping that everything will finally turn out for the best.

When you go in the wrong direction, your strategy and budget will show you and help get you back on the right track.

3) Treat your customers well, but don't give the store away. And while this allows you to adjust the way you do business right now; you need to be responsive to customer needs.

Be aware, however, that you are not putting your profit opportunity at risk by listening to their comments and doing what you can to make them happy.

In every transaction with a client, you must be able to make a profit regardless of the amount invested.

4) Last, but certainly not least, enjoy yourself. You started your own business so that you could be your own boss and stay away from the stiff and proper corporate world. Make your business a fun place to work.

Even if you are not exactly able to achieve the goals that you set, take advantage of whatever success you can achieve.

This book and the stories it contain are about the journey of the Third Age business owners who chose to change their lives question and transcend the Social Convention.

Along with the array of questions and opinions, it is believed that you have internalized quite a few perspectives.

At a certain point, these people give us their services, their goods, but above all they give us inspiration.

Our entrepreneurs are accomplished individuals who, because they meant it, knew the constraints of being on the second part of their adult life but were able to resolve it. Numerous factors, personal, economics or their beliefs motivated them to become successful despite the odds.

Last but not the least, have fun; make it a fun place to work for your business. Get excited about yourself and the people who work with you and question them.

Hope you enjoyed our virtual journey of talking to you and writing about yourself.

This is your start

It's time to roll up your sleeves and get started, now that you understand what you need.

I wish you lots of luck and wealth.

www.ingramcontent.com/pod-product-compliance
Lightning Source LLC
Chambersburg PA
CBHW031430210526
45464CB00005B/2131